Ceramic Tile Setting

John P. Bridge

Photography by Robert A. Bedient

TAB BOOKS

Blue Ridge Summit, PA

FIRST EDITION
FIRST PRINTING

© 1992 by **TAB Books**.
TAB Books is a division of McGraw-Hill, Inc.

Library of Congress Cataloging-in-Publication Data

Bridge, John P.
    Ceramic tile setting / by John P. Bridge ; photography by Robert
A. Bedient.
      p.   cm.
    Includes index.
    ISBN 0-8306-2573-9 (h)   ISBN 0-8306-2572-0 (p)
    1. Tile laying—Amateurs' manuals.   I. Title.
TH8531.B75   1992
693'.3—dc20   91-44200
                                   CIP

TAB Books offers software for sale. For information and a catalog, please contact TAB Software Department, Blue Ridge Summit, PA 17294-0850.

Book Editor: Lori Flaherty
Book Design: Jaclyn J. Boone
Director of Production: Katherine G. Brown
Cover Design: Lori E. Schlosser   TAB1

Contents

PART 2
CERAMIC TILE FLOORS

Acknowledgments

My sincere thanks to Larry Ross and Barney Stump of Bowman Tile Supply, Houston, Texas, for reviewing and contributing the tile distributor's point of view to this work.

I would also like to express my gratitude to Carol Bedient for reviewing and proofreading the manuscript.

Finally, I owe an unpayable debt to the people at TAB Books, particularly Stacy Pomeroy and Lori Flaherty, for turning my scribbling into sensible reading.

Introduction

As a ceramic tile setter, particularly as a contractor dealing with homeowners during the past decade, I've perceived a real need for a concise, comprehensive book on tile setting for the do-it-yourselfer. The shelves of book stores and libraries are overflowing with volumes on woodworking, plumbing, carpentry, and electrical wiring. Little exists on ceramic tile installation, and much of what does is incomplete and, in some cases, misleading.

This book is for people contemplating doing their own tile work or for those who plan on contracting the work out. It will provide some insight on what you can expect for your money. What's the best way to build a tile tub surround? How should ceramic tile floors be installed? Which tiles and materials should be used on a project? And exactly what is a ceramic tile setter; what does he do to earn his keep?

As many of you have undoubtedly done, I've read countless magazine articles that attempt to teach the do-it-yourselfer the tricks and techniques of proper tile installation. But there isn't enough room in a magazine article (or the whole magazine, for that matter), to provide enough information to carry out a somewhat complex project and bring it to a satisfactory conclusion. In addition to the dos and don'ts, we need to know the whys and why nots. And we need some background on the tile setter's trade so that we can fully appreciate what the undertaking entails.

The tools of the carpenter, the plumber, and the electrician are common to most home do-it-yourselfers, but those of the mason and the tile setter are not. They are foreign and mysterious to us, though they are generally basic and easy to use once we gain familiarity with them.

Ceramic tile projects, unless they are very small, are expensive. And you usually get only one chance to do a proper job. Cement is a somewhat permanent and unforgiving material. It doesn't lend itself to disassembly as do the materials used in carpentry, for example. It is of no consequence to nail up a board and later notice that it's a bit long. You simply take it down, saw it off a little, and nail it back up. Try that with ceramic tile set in a portland cement-base material and it'll soon be apparent that you possibly should have known a little more about what you were doing before you began!

The tile setter spends much of his time "laying out" his project. You'll see him standing around, looking up, down, and around. To the uninitiated, it would seem he's not doing much of anything (which is sometimes the case). But generally, he's sizing up the job and trying to determine the best possible way to bring it to fruitation. Before he installs the first piece of material, he has to know where the last piece is going to end up and how it's going to look. He's responsible not only for completing the job in a manner that is workmanlike and technically correct, it also has to look right. As in other trades concerned with the finished aspect of construction, if it doesn't look right, it's wrong! It's impossible to place too much emphasis on the importance of taking the time to contemplate a project and visualize the way it's going to look when it is completed.

Over the years, many new and innovative materials have arrived on the scene; some good, some not so good. If we were to believe the promises of the manufacturers, we would assume that all new products are better than the old standbys, when in fact, some of them are "better" simply because they are inexpensive and easier to produce. I'm not one to shun new methods and materials. Some of them have revolutionized the tile setting industry and made our job easier, which is wonderful, so long as we don't have to give up quality workmanship. Years ago, it was necessary to soak tiles in water so that they would adhere to the portland cement slurry that was used to attach them. The process was messy and labor-intensive. With the advent of thin set mortar, this became unnecessary, and the same amount of work could be done in much less time. Thin set is every bit as good as pure cement, and in most cases, even stronger. Unfortunately, this is not true of many of the newer materials now in use.

Can you do the work? I fully believe that anyone with normal manual dexterity, given enough time, the necessary tools, and proper instruction, can come up with a satisfactory job. Different levels of skill are required for different applications. For example, installing tile on floors is easier than installing it on walls. Gravity is working to your advantage and the tile stays more or less where it is put. On walls, it has to be supported by some means or another if it is expected to stay in place. A person who is comfortable doing a bathroom floor might not be up to tiling a tub surround. We learn by doing and each job well done instills in us a little more confidence.

It is my aim to provide enough information to enable you to select your own level of skill. I will endeavor to acquaint you with the basic fundamentals as well as some of the "tricks" of the trade as we go along. Although this book is not intended as a manual for the professional tile setter, it contains enough material to enable you to do many of the things a tile setter does.

No one person's approach or solution to a problem should be considered to be the final one—including my own. Opinions on how to install tile are as varied as the tile setters plying their craft. Advice offered by anyone in the trade should be sought and listened to. Tile setters (good ones, that is) are not overly concerned with job security and are usually more than willing to give tips and pointers.

Although their opinions sometimes differ from those of the tile installer, manufacturers and distributors can be a good source of information. When I say distributors, I'm referring to the people whose main business is selling ceramic tile and marble products. Chain and discount stores don't usually employ people who have a special knowledge of any one product because there are too many products to be familiar with, although they might have you believe otherwise. So when you need special information, ask a specialist. Many of the people who work in tile supply stores have, at one time or another, been involved in installation. Ask as many questions as you can, and before long, you'll be forming your own opinions.

There are few things in life as satisfying as having completed a project with your own hands; one that you can be proud of; one that you can show your friends and neighbors, and bask in the glory of their praise . . . especially if it's one that is a bit more complex than the ordinary. On the other hand, there is nothing more disheartening than a job that doesn't turn out well. So take your time. After all, time is on your side . . . you're not getting paid for it anyway. Get your facts straight before you begin, and most of all . . . enjoy yourself!

To Patti, my wife and helper.

How to use this book

*T*his book is divided into projects, or I should say, groups of projects, and I have attempted to arrange them in respect to their degree of difficulty. At the same time, this is not a "project book." Rather, it must be considered as a whole. Project books assume a certain knowledge on the part of the reader. Because very little has been written on installing ceramic tile, that foreknowledge does not exist. So other than assuming the reader is familiar with common tools found around the house, I make no assumptions.

It is therefore necessary to read from the front and "build up" to the project that interests you. A carpenter cannot be expected to frame a floor without knowing something about foundations and walls. In this respect, a tile setter, or any craftsman, is trained in stages, and each progressive stage is intrinsic to the one following it. In Part 1, you'll learn about all of the materials and tools used in setting ceramic tile and their qualities as well as how to choose the best tile for the job. Part 2 on installing ceramic floors is especially important, regardless of whether you plan on tiling a floor, because it covers the basics of mixing cement mortar, building the all-important screed, squaring and centering tiles, and other pertinent information.

I've attempted to convey my message in as few words as possible, and at the same time, make the reading enjoyable. Most projects in this book require the services of a helper. You can go it alone, but it's tough. A professional seldom works without a helper, and in the tile trade, the two are referred to as a crew. A helper absolutely makes or breaks a tile setter.

In the home, the helper is often the spouse, and I think this is a great way to go—keep it in the family. On several occasions, I've had small, out of town jobs, usually on weekends where it doesn't pay to employ a helper. Because all expenses are paid by the company I contract to, I came up with a brainstorm (worthy of mention, I might add, because it doesn't happen that often). Why not take my wife, Patti, out of town with me? Surely, she'd be a great deal of help, and it would certainly beat spending the night alone in a strange motel room. I mean, the mental light bulbs were really flashing.

After agreeing to accompany me, she promptly informed me that she would have to be paid. "Why?" I asked, "all the money comes into the house anyway." "Because if I'm going to work, I'm going to be paid," she said. "How much?" I asked. "As much as you pay your regular helper, " she replied.

"But he's experienced."

"Then take him."

So much for labor-management relations. We arrived at the job Saturday afternoon. My plan was to set the tile, go to bed, grout early in the morning, and get home in time for the second football game. With a little help, I could get the tile set in four or five hours and take the rest of the evening off.

First, I helped Patti unload the tile from the truck. Then I helped her get a couple buckets of water. I asked her to unload the grout and thin set and get it into the building. It turned out that she could carry two 25-pound sacks of grout, but not one 50-pound sack of thin set. I carried the thin set. I mixed the thin set. Patti held one end of the chalk line when we laid out the floor.

We finished setting tile about one o'clock in the morning and went to bed. Patti said we would have finished much sooner had I not stood around so much. The next morning, we grouted the floor. We had thin set left over that had to be loaded back onto the truck.

Needless to say, I fell asleep during the second football game.

A few days later, Patti demanded her pay. "You've got the check-book, write yourself a check," I told her. "Oh no, you've got to pay me," she said. The next day, I cashed a check and paid her.

Would I take her again? Naturally. It beat spending the night alone in a strange motel room.

TILES, TOOLS, AND MATERIALS

The craft of the tile setter and that of the mason have gone hand in hand since tile was first produced, about four thousand years before the birth of Christ. Of the skilled trades, masonry is the oldest profession; well, maybe the second oldest profession. In any case, the separate craft of tile setting came into being much later, probably during the Renaissance. In ancient times, tiles were usually installed by the masons of the day or by the artisans who fashioned them.

Decorative ceramic tiles were first used in Egypt to adorn tombs and the palaces of the Pharaohs. At the same time, the tile making art was gradually spreading throughout the Middle East, and later, to Northern Europe. It seems Persia was responsible for developing the skills and techniques that were later employed on the European continent. Tiles were brought to Iberia (Spain) from North Africa by the Moors and the Crusaders.

From the Iberian peninsula, decorative tiles were carried to the New World on the ships of the conquistadores, where they adorned the walls of newly built churches and missions.

Finally, having made their way to our country, mainly from Northern Europe, tiles were used to decorate the halls and chambers of the wealthy. At this time, they were still too expensive to be used in utilitarian applications.

Today, although still decorative, ceramic tiles are used in

an infinite number of ways. They are no longer exclusively in the domain of the wealthy but are a common sight in almost every American household and office building. In industry, where walls and floors must be durable and easily cleaned, tiles are a favored option.

The art of setting tile has changed little since ancient times. The most prominent event that comes to mind is the invention of cement mortar by the Romans. New and improved materials have been incorporated, but the installation of ceramic tile is, to this day, a hand-operated, labor-intensive process. With the advent of modular construction in homes and other buildings, mass methods of installation are being experimented with, but to date, none has been appreciably successful. The professional tile setter can go his merry way, secure in the knowledge that he's not going to be replaced by a machine in the foreseeable future.

Chapter **1**

Materials and their uses

*T*ile setters are much like masons, and many of the materials used in the trade are common. But it seems that cement mortar, which has been around for at least a thousand years, is still a mystery to many home do-it-yourselfer's. When I attended high school, there were classes in woodworking, metalworking, printing, and auto mechanics. Masonry projects, however, are not very portable and don't lend themselves to classroom or shop instruction. I did, however, gain vast experience in the art of turning wooden bowls on the lathe, and some of my counterparts in the metal shop became experts at making knives and billy clubs.

Aside from common masonry materials, there are a number of products that are peculiar to the tile setting trade, and I'll discuss them briefly. Let's start with cement, because it is the basic ingredient of mortar and other materials.

CEMENTS

In the tile trade, cement is mainly used for making mortar, although it does have other uses. There are various types of cement, all formulated for specific uses. We'll deal with only a few of them as we go along.

Portland cement

Portland cement, the most common cement used in construction, is made by combining limestone, clay, and other elements which are then "cooked" in an oven, or kiln. The resultant "clinkers" are then pulverized into a fine powder. The name *portland* is derived from the town of

Portland, England, the color of whose building stone, the material approximates. The word *portland* has long been a trade term and has nothing to do with the brand or origin of the product.

When the process for making portland cement was perfected some 100 years ago, the material was referred to as *artificial cement* (as opposed to natural cement, which had been used previously). Natural cement was, and is, in some countries, produced by locating stone that contains the necessary elements in more or less the correct proportions. As you can guess, it is a hit and miss concept, and the resulting material is inconsistent from one batch to the next.

Portland cement, however, is produced by refining the ingredients and bringing them together in exact proportions; hence, the term *artificial*. It seems, in the old days, the problem was one of transportation, and when modern means of transport became available, the production of better material became practical.

Masonry cement

Masonry cement, also called masonry mix, is portland cement to which lime, and sometimes latex, has been added. It's convenient to use when making mortar because you just add sand and water. It's also much easier to lift. It comes in 70-pound sacks, whereas portland comes in 94-pound sacks.

MORTARS

Mortar is made by combining portland cement, lime, sand, and water. In tile work, it is normally troweled or floated onto a surface, such as a wall, and then smoothed flat so that tile can later be set over it. It is now a substrate—a word you'll be seeing often in booklets and on the labels of products. The substrate is simply whatever happens to be under the tiles as they're set, be it mortar, wood, wallboard, or concrete. Mortar containing lime is often referred to as "fat mud."

Floor mud

Mortar used to float horizontal surfaces, such as floors and countertops, does not contain lime, because it isn't needed to hold the mud together. Gravity does that job. This type of mortar is called "floor mud" or "deck mud." In certain areas of the country, it is referred to as "dry pack." It contains very little water; just enough to activate the cement.

Construction lime

Construction lime is an industrial form of calcium oxide that is added to mortar to give it "cling." Without lime, it would not be practical to trowel mortar onto vertical surfaces. Construction lime is available in 50-pound sacks from masonry suppliers.

Synthetic wall mud

Synthetic wall mud, an alternative to conventional mortar, contains a lightweight aggregate in place of sand. It is available in 50-pound sacks at most tile suppliers.

Thin set (dry set)

Thin set is the material most often used for actually attaching tiles. It is made from portland cement and other ingredients that seem to be trade secrets. No matter, you don't have to know what's in it to know that it works and works well. It's the best thing that has come along in years. Although there are many brands of thin set, there are only two basic types: one for walls, which is usually white, and one for floors, which is gray like cement.

Thin set is usually used to attach tiles to mortar or concrete and sometimes drywall (sheetrock). If you're laying tiles over wood, you'll need thin set that is labeled "Multipurpose" or "Multi-cure."

Latex

In the tile trade, latex refers to a white, watery mixture that resembles milk and comes either in gallon jugs or five-gallon buckets. It is used as an additive to various cement products. When mixed with thin set, the resulting material becomes stronger and more water-resistant than regular thin set. I use latex often on outdoor projects that will be exposed to the elements. It is also used as a grout additive to make grout stronger and more elastic. Although latex is generally not needed inside the home, it can be mixed with pure cement and used as a filler for small depressions in floors and other surfaces.

Grout

Grout is the material that goes between the tiles and is basically just cement. It comes in white and a variety of premixed colors. Grouts used on floors, or when the tile joints are wider than one-eighth of an inch, contain silica sand for a measure of added strength.

OTHER ADHESIVES
Mastic

There are a number of products on the market that fall into the mastic group. Mastics are not used in "mud work" but over surfaces such as drywall, wood, plastic (Formica), and metal. Although thin set is stronger and more durable, there are times when it won't work and mastic is needed. I don't recommend its use directly over wood floors, or any floor. I believe that tile installed on floors should be set over a masonry substrate. Manufacturers, distributors, and some tile installers might say otherwise, however.

Epoxy

Epoxy has few applications in residential work, and most professional tile setters consider its use a classic case of overkill. It's also very expensive. Epoxy is often specified for commercial and industrial applications, especially on government jobs where cost doesn't seem to be a factor. The price of many new epoxy grouts on the market is eight to ten times the price of portland cement grout. However, these new epoxy grouts are purported to be stain-proof, and standard grouts are not, even if they're sealed. Also, the washing during installation is done with water rather than a solvent—a definite plus. If you're interested, ask about them at your tile supply store.

METAL LATH

An expanded metal lath is used to reinforce mortar when it is applied to walls and floors. Chicken wire (poultry netting) can also be used. These and other materials are discussed further as we proceed with the projects.

By now, you've probably realized that I'm a "mud man." I like to do things the old-fashioned way simply because I'm convinced that those methods are the best . . . they've withstood the test of time. I incorporate new materials and techniques only when they have been proven to be as good or better than the ones that have endured through the years. But, I guarantee my workmanship for life; mine or my customer's, whichever ends first. I make this guaranty daily, and seldom do I have to return to a job to make repairs. I am extremely proud of the work I do, and I won't allow it to be tainted by inferior materials or methods.

Chapter **2**

Tools of
the trade

Many of the tools used in tile setting are common, and you probably have some of them around the house. Others are not so common, and you'll need to borrow, rent, or purchase them. This chapter covers the tools needed for most projects. Included is a brief description of each and an explanation of its use. All of the tools won't be needed for each project, so don't run out and buy anything just yet. See FIG. 1-1.

ALIGNMENT TOOLS
Levels

Levels, sometimes called *spirit levels*, are made in several different ways and of various materials; generally, wood, metal, or plastic. A 4-foot level is recommended, although a 2-foot level will do if it's used in conjunction with a 4- or 5-foot straightedge. Tile setters usually carry both.

Levels with fixed vials (the tube with the bubble in it) are best. Vials attached with screws, or so-called "adjustable levels," tend to adjust themselves out of level more often than not. Masons and tile setters usually prefer levels made of wood with metal edges. Levels take a beating, so the money spent on a good one won't be wasted.

Straightedges

Straightedges are used for scraping mortar smooth and flat, checking the straightness of walls and floors, and many other functions. Good quality metal straightedges are available but common wood boards work just as well.

Boards purchased as straightedges should be straight-grained, with few or no knots. A 1 × 4 makes a good straightedge and is convenient to handle. Straightedges will often be wet, so pick boards that won't warp or twist.

Steel square

A standard framing square is useful (but not essential) for some projects. You won't be using the numbered scales, so an inexpensive one is fine as long as it is truly square. Smaller versions also work.

Float strips

Float strips are nothing more than lengths of wood lattice that are tapped into wet mortar with a level. They are used to get a wall plumb, or vertical. Float strips are discussed further as the need for them arises.

CEMENT TOOLS
Mortar board (mud board)

A mortar board is a piece of 1/2- or 3/4-inch plywood, about 30 inches square, used to hold mortar at a convenient height while floating walls. Some sort of stand must be rigged to hold it up. There are many ingenious ways of doing this, and I'll cover a few of them later.

Hawk

A hawk is a small metal platform about 14 inches square with a handle under it. It is used to hold mortar in one hand while troweling it on a wall with a flat trowel held in the other hand. Sounds like real fun, doesn't it?

I-I From the top (clockwise): tile cutter, notched trowel, biters, grout float, margin trowel, buttering (gauging) trowel, flat trowel.

Flat trowel

A flat trowel is used to trowel mortar on a wall and for applying "mud" to "floated" surfaces such as floors and countertops. Flat trowels come in many sizes, but the one you'll need is 4 or 5 inches wide by 12 inches long. You won't need any of the longer ones, which are used primarily in cement finishing.

Pointing trowel

A pointing trowel, or pointer, is used to get into corners where no other tool will reach. Some tile setters don't use one, but use a margin trowel, a sharp stick, or their finger. If you buy a pointer, get a small one. Don't end up with a mason's trowel, a monstrous affair that has no use in tile work.

Margin trowel

The margin trowel is invaluable. It is used in "mud work" for getting into tight places where a flat trowel won't reach. It consists of a wooden handle with a small rectangular blade protruding from its end. It's also handy for scraping mud out of buckets and a variety of other uses. Buy a 6-inch margin trowel, it is the most common in tile work.

Buttering trowel

The buttering trowel, also referred to as the gauging trowel or tile setter's trowel, is one of the most-used tools in the trade. It is similar to the margin trowel but has a larger, trapezoid-shaped blade. The end is rounded, and it's handy for buttering thin set onto the backs of tiles and for digging mud out of buckets. Some tile setters use a well worn and rounded margin trowel instead.

Notched trowel

A notched trowel is similar to a flat trowel. Its edges have notches to help spread thin set and other adhesives onto surfaces to be tiled. There are different size notched trowels for different applications.

NOTE: When buying trowels, or any tool, buy professional quality ones. Cheaper trowels don't flex well, the handles tend to fall off, and the blades rust. Good tools are expensive, but they're worth the investment.

Mixing box

A mixing box is a large metal trough that mortar is mixed in. You could make a mixing box out of wood or sheet metal but they are harder to use and are considered a one-time affair. A wheelbarrow can be used for mixing mud, especially when you have only a small amount to mix.

Electric or gasoline-powered mixers are most often used only on large jobs where a great deal of mud is needed. On small jobs, they're a complete waste of time because it takes so long to clean them. Resign ourself to mixing your own mud by hand; another reason to employ a helper.

Masonry hoe

The masonry hoe, a larger version of the basic garden hoe, is used, along with the mixing box or wheelbarrow, to mix mortar. It has a long handle and an oversized blade and is the tool of choice for mixing large amounts of mortar. If you need only mix a small amount of mortar, a garden hoe will do the job.

Shovel

Although any shovel will work for tile setting, a square-bladed cement shovel works best. Its flat blade makes it easy to pick up sand or mortar, whereas a round-bladed shovel leaves something to be desired.

Grout float

After tile is installed, it is grouted by smearing grout over the entire surface of the tile and squeezing it into the joints. A rubber grout float is the best tool to use for this job. You'll find it anyplace masonry tools are sold, or you might be able to borrow one from your tile supplier.

CUTTING TOOLS

Tile cutter

A tile cutter, or cutting board, is indispensable in tile work. There are many sizes and styles on the market. Through the years, the workhorse of many tile setters has been the Superior No. 2. It accommodates tiles up to about 10 inches square and is not hard to use once you have the feel of it.

It might not be necessary to buy a cutter, because many tile suppliers loan or rent them to their customers. The tool is manually operated, and the process is similar to cutting glass. A scoring wheel is drawn across the face of the tile, and the piece is then snapped in two. After a little practice, you'll be cutting tile like a pro. Large cutters are available for bigger tiles.

Nippers

Nippers, biters, or nibblers are hand tools resembling pliers except that they have carbide cutting edges embedded in their jaws. They are used to make small, irregular cuts by biting off bits of tile such as around a shower head or other obstacle. Biters can be borrowed or rented, but if you're doing a lot of work, you should have your own, they'll be sharper.

Tile saw

Tile saws are used for making L-shaped, U-shaped, and other shaped cuts that are difficult to make with a tile cutter and biters. The principle of operation of a tile saw is simple. Water (for cooling) is pumped over a circular blade whose edges are encrusted with industrial diamond chips. The tile is fed under the blade on a rolling table.

It's sometimes possible to lay out small floors such as baths and entryways so that no L cuts are needed, but I'm afraid this is not usually the case. You'll most likely need a saw when doing floor work for getting around cabinet bases and getting into doorways.

For some reason, tile and masonry saws are extremely expensive. You can buy a top-notch contractor's table saw for woodworking, which is much more sophisticated, for less than the cost of a fairly unsophisticated tile saw. One company that manufactured them for many years, was recently bought out by another long-standing saw manufacturing company. Perhaps this is why they're so dear. In any case, you won't be buying a tile saw.

Tile saws can be rented at rental yards, but some yards require that the blade be rented separately or that you actually buy the blade, which can cost anywhere from $80 to $150. Fortunately, most good tile suppliers have ''wet saws,'' which are permanently set up for their customer's use. In this case, you could lay an entire floor leaving the L cuts for last, then marking the tile carefully and carting it to the supplier for cutting. Of course, if you're not careful, you'll be making more than one trip.

Tin snips

Tin snips are used only for cutting metal lath or chicken wire (poultry netting). Large tin snips are more convenient than smaller ones for cutting metal lath, but "aviation" or sheet metal snips will also do the job.

Masonry chisel

Similar to a cold chisel, the mason's chisel has a wide flat blade. It's used to chop up old tile, remove small humps from concrete floors, and a variety of other tasks. A chisel with a blade of about $1^1/2$ inches in width will do almost any job, although a cold chisel might also work well.

ACCESSORY TOOLS
Beating block

A beating block is a flat block that is held in the hand, flat against tiles that are being set in mortar, and struck on the backside with a hammer or trowel handle to get tiles flush. It is also used to float or smooth mortar that has partially set. Manufactured beating blocks are available but a flat piece of wood works just as well. Your beating block should be 4 or 5 inches in width and about 7 or 8 inches long.

Rubbing stone

Similar in appearance to a sharpening stone, a rubbing stone is used to smooth the sharp edges of cut tiles. Most cuts are made in corners or against a wall or a floor, but occasionally, pieces must be set where the cut is exposed. This is when the stone is used.

Measuring tape or rule

Some craftmen still prefer the old folding measuring rule, (maybe it's a status symbol), but I've found that a metal measuring tape is more convenient to use, especially when laying out floors. Mine is 25 feet long. I like it because it's rigid enough to push out along the floor without kinking.

Knee pads

If you're going to be doing any amount of floor work, you'll come to absolutely love knee pads. If you can't find them at your local hardware or home center store, they're always available at tile and masonry supply stores.

Chalk line

A chalk line or chalk box is used in making straight lines on floors. Any color of chalk can be used, but blue and red are most favored by professionals because they show up well on surfaces.

Buckets

You simply can't have enough buckets. Buckets for water, thin set, mortar, grout, and any number of materials used in tile setting are needed. The most useful are large plastic ones that paint, pickles, drywall compound, and other materials and products come in.

Keep your buckets clean. I know it's hard after a long day to take the time to clean things up for the next day, but it's part of the trade, and it's one of the reasons I employ a helper or two. Metal buckets are of little use and shouldn't be bothered with. They're too hard to clean for reuse.

Sponges

Although it might seem like an insignificant item, a sponge is one of the main tools used in the tile trade. Tile setters don't work without a bucket of water with a sponge in it nearby. All of the tools we've discussed must be kept clean. Cement products will permanently encrust them if they're not washed frequently. Also, sponges are used to keep the tile clean as it is being installed, as well as for cleaning grout from tiled surfaces. Buy two or three of the largest sponges you can find from your tile supplier. Sponges bought in retail stores usually won't do the job as well.

I'm sure there are many other tools and accessories that could be used in the course of setting tile. But many of them can be made from available materials. I've seen all manner of contrivances that work well. Not every tool mentioned here will be needed. It depends on the scope of the work to be done. So, don't purchase anything until you're sure there's no other way to go.

It is a good idea to buy tools where the professionals buy theirs. Tradesmen, who have to make their living using them, won't buy inferior tools. For this reason, you'll find only the best at tile and masonry supply stores. A good craftsman is proud of his tools, and won't have anything laying around to be ashamed of or that might produce inferior results. Who knows when another craftsman might arrive on the scene?

Chapter **3**

Types of tile

*T*his chapter does not cover the processes that go into producing ceramic tile in-depth, but rather their characteristics. Are the tiles hard and durable enough to use in a high-traffic area such as an entryway? Can they be easily cleaned? What type of tile works well on kitchen counters? How about outdoors?

The term, *ceramic tile*, is a broad one, and many varieties of tile fall into this category. Usually, when we hear the word ceramic, we think of figurines and various other doodads, and we're not far off the mark. Ceramic wall tiles, those generally used in showers and tub surrounds, are made much the same way as figurines. The body of the piece, or bisque, is formed from semiliquid clay and then fired in a kiln at moderate temperatures. The bisque is decorated by any of a number of means, glazed, and then re-fired. This produces a bright, durable surface that will last a long time . . . forever, if properly cared for. And it looks great, but it wouldn't last long on an entryway floor.

There are tiles made specifically for high-traffic areas that are as bright and as beautiful as wall tiles. They are made by an entirely different process but they are also called ceramic tiles. This chapter covers most of the tiles you'll run into, as well as their properties and uses.

STANDARD WALL TILES

Any type of tile can be put on a wall. It simply will not receive the type of abuse it would on a floor. But for many years, tile has been made in exactly the same size: 4¼ inches square. It's called *standard wall tile*, and in our trade, it's referred to as "four-and-a-quarter." Although some companies, for reasons not known to me, make theirs slightly larger—4³/8 inches square.

Shapes, or trim pieces, are produced in matching colors and textures for all domestically made standard wall tile and are identified by a numbering system. Included are *bullnose* pieces, or caps, which are used to round over a tiled surface; and *coves*, which can be used to round out the juncture of a wall and floor, for example. There are many other shapes that can be used in almost any situation.

Standard wall tile is also made in a 6-×-6-inch size for which the same trim pieces are used. Four-and-a-quarter is the tile most often seen in the residential bathroom. It is relatively easy to install because the tiles have spacer lugs, which support them as they are laid up or set, molded into their edges.

MOSAIC TILES

Mosaic tile includes any tile that is less than 2 inches square, although they might be round or hexagonal. Mosaic tiles can be either glazed or unglazed, and they're usually mounted on 12-×-12-inch sheets of backing, which might be of perforated paper, plastic, rubber, or cloth netting.

Mosaics are usually made of porcelain, although a few are ceramic. If you have a ceramic tile shower in your home, the floor might be covered with mosaics. In some homes, the entire bathroom might be done in porcelain mosaics, but to me, they look commercial. In fact, you'll see them in almost every commercial restroom covering the floors and the walls.

Porcelain mosaics are extremely durable, frost-proof, and a good choice for any application, including kitchen countertops. In the case of unglazed tiles, the color goes all the way through the piece, so it'll never wear out. Trim pieces are available for most mosaic tiles.

QUARRY TILES

For years, the floors in commercial kitchens, butcher shops, and other facilities, have been covered with quarry tile. They are durable and relatively inexpensive. Quarry tile is made of natural clay, and in many cases, the color of the clay determines the color of the tile. Some of them are multicolored and contain marblelike swirls or patterns resembling wood grain.

Although quarry tile is used extensively in commercial applications, it is gaining popularity in the home—inside and out. The tones are "earthy" and lend a contemporary look to floors. A good many of them are flashed, meaning the shades vary. Flashed tiles complement a country or rustic decor.

Because quarry tile is made much like brick, it is sometimes referred to as "burnt clay." The most common size is 6 × 6 inches, although there are other sizes and shapes. They are available in a range of shapes, including the basic square, the rectangle (brick), and the hexagon. They are frost-proof, and are a good choice for outdoor projects.

BRICK PAVERS AND PAVER TILES

Brick pavers look like bricks that have been turned sideways and then sawn in half. They are about 1-inch thick and come in all the colors that bricks are made in. Once installed, paver tiles look the same as brick pavers but they're about half as thick.

Members of the "burnt clay" family, pavers and paver tiles are durable and frost-proof. The nominal size for both is 4 × 8 inches. Nosings are used on the front of stair treads and around swimming pools. Because pavers and paver tiles are used primarily on floors and decks, other trims are not usually available.

GLAZED FLOOR TILES

In homes where tile is the floor covering of choice, glazed floor tiles are the beauties that grace the vast majority of them. The range of color and texture is limitless, and they come in enough sizes and shapes to suit the most discriminating decorator. There are squares, rectangles, hexagons, octagons, and various shapes that defy description. In fact, I've had customers complain that there are just too many to choose from.

Although a few companies in the United States produce glazed floor tiles, most of them come from other countries, particularly the European continent. Italy has long been a leader in manufacturing and exporting glazed floor tile, and Spain is not far behind.

Other European countries supplying ceramic tiles to the United States include Germany, France, Portugal, and England. Lately, I've noticed quality floor tiles coming out of Mexico, and several South American countries have long been in the business.

Although the country of origin has little to do with the quality of the tile, the methods used to produce it certainly do. There are various ways of making floor tiles, but I'll group them into only two categories: single-fired and multi-fired. Single-fired tiles are the ones you should consider because they are the most durable.

In single-fired tiles, the bisque is colored and glazed before it is "cooked" in a kiln at extremely high temperatures, usually 1200 to 1500 degrees Fahrenheit. The result is hard tile, resilient enough to last a lifetime—and longer. Because of the extreme temperatures, there is a certain amount of distortion, and the only way of controlling it is by grading the tiles by size after they've left the kiln. Therefore, it is important to ensure that your tiles are all from the same lot.

In the United States, floor tiles, foreign ones included, are graded according to their resistance to abrasion. The grades are numbered I through IV, with grade IV being the most resistant. This information is usually not on the packaging, so you'll have to depend on your tile supplier to provide it—another good reason to stick with a professional supplier. In residential applications, grade III is more than adequate for any traffic area, and grade II might be considered for areas that won't receive the brunt of traffic.

Multi-fired tiles, even triple-fired tiles, should not be used on floors where heavy traffic is anticipated. They are fired at lower temperatures, and the clay is not as dense as that used in the single-firing method. The glazes, which are not as well bonded as those of single-fired tiles, tend to chip more readily. So, if you want a floor that's going to last indefinitely, choose a more durable tile.

SALTILLO TILES (SAL-TEÉ-OH)

Saltillo tile, often called Mexican tile, derives its name from the town of Saltillo, Mexico, where it is made by hand from raw clay. The process is similar to that used in biblical times when clay tiles were first known to have been produced. The tiles are dried in the sun and are soft and crumble easily.

It seems that people who like Saltillo, absolutely love it, and those who don't, hate it. There's no middle ground. I like the rustic look of it, but I don't think I'd like to live with it in my home. I really like it when used outdoors, although it's not frost-proof (so don't any of you Yankees try putting it out on your patio). When used indoors, it's almost always finished with a top coat similar to that used on hardwood floors, so it's not exactly maintenance-free. In areas of the United States that border Mexico, Saltillo floors are common.

TERRA-COTTA TILES

Terra-cotta, Italian for "cooked earth," is actually semi-cooked. Terra cotta tile is made from raw clay and is usually unglazed. The colors range from gray and brownish yellow to various shades of red. When used indoors, it can be left raw, but more often, it is finished with a top coat. Some terra-cotta tiles are purported to be waterproof, but I've never handled any that are. To the contrary, the terra-cottas I've installed are like sponges when it comes to soaking up water. They are, however, beautiful, and they lend an informal air to residential floors.

CEMENT TILES

As the name implies, cement is the main material used to manufacture cement tiles. Most of them are pigmented to give them an "earthy" look similar to terra-cotta tile. Cement tiles are produced extensively in the United States and other countries. They are used primarily indoors because they're not frost-proof, and they are usually finished with a top coat.

PORCELAIN-GRANITE TILES

Porcelain-granite tiles, made by a process similar to mosaic tiles, are difficult to distinguish from natural granite once installed. And in many cases, they are more durable than the real thing! Being "rock hard," they are hard to cut. They wear out cutting tools faster than anything else I've installed.

Because they are very dense, porcelainized granite tiles are almost completely waterproof and frost-proof. They come in several sizes, and the available finishes include slate, matte, and polished. They are relatively expensive. The polished ones cost as much or more than real granite. Although they are used mainly in commercial applications, these tiles are definitely suitable for use in the home.

SWIMMING POOL TILES

Imported almost exclusively from Japan, pool tiles are in a class of their own. They are made of glazed porcelain and are waterproof and frost-proof. Like mosaics, they are usually mounted on sheets of backing. They come in an infinite variety of shapes and colors, and they are highly decorative.

You'll find Japanese pool tiles around the water line of almost every in-ground pool in the country. I've used them to add decorative borders to tub surrounds, shower stalls, and wainscots.

GLAZED PORCELAIN TILES

Porcelain is a stronger material than most ceramic clays, and porcelain tiles might be considered an alternative to standard ceramic wall tiles. They come in various sizes, colors, and shapes. Along with mosaics, they are suitable for use almost anywhere—countertops, tub surrounds, showers, floors—anyplace you can think of. Like mosaics, they're usually, but not always, mounted on sheets for ease of installation.

One drawback, if it can be considered that, is that porcelain tiles are generally not uniform in size. They're cooked at very high temperatures, which, as I mentioned earlier, causes distortion. Therefore, the "look" is not as regimental as it would be using standard wall tiles.

Porcelain glazes can be bright and glossy or matted. Some of the pieces seem to be almost translucent. As is the case with pool tiles, glazed porcelain tiles are usually made in Japan and other Asian countries.

Although I know I've covered the basics, with the range of materials available to us, I'm sure I've forgotten something. Or, perish the thought, there might be something I don't know about! But entire books have been written about each of the types of tile discussed here, and new tiles arrive on the scene almost daily. Finally, we have better things to do. So let's actually do something.

DESIGN

Before you rush out to buy your tile, a word about design is in order. The work you're doing is permanent and can't be easily changed the way drapes or wallpaper can be. If you're never going to sell your house, you can do anything that pleases you, without regard for the preferences of others. You can do what you please, anyway; it's your house, but if you might someday want to put it on the market, you should consider creating an improvement that will aid the sale, rather than hinder it.

The current trend in interior design is to leave the floors somewhat muted, not overdone with pattern and color. Many professional designers would rather add pattern and color to walls, drapes, and furnishings and leave the floors neutral. How often might you want to redecorate? And what if you just get tired of looking at a pattern or bright color? I don't claim to be a designer, but I do recommend you stick with something you can live with for years to come.

Part 2

CERAMIC TILE FLOORS

In choosing ceramic tile for your floor, you've made an excellent decision, and you're joining countless other homeowners who have opted for floors that are beautiful and durable. In fact, when properly installed and cared for, a tile floor will hold up indefinitely. When ease of maintenance is considered, tile has to be at the very top of the list. Most glazed floor tiles need be only cleaned with water; a little ammonia, added to the water, helps eliminate streaking.

Then there is the matter of cost. Ceramic tile is expensive, but then again, so are other floor coverings. Although tile prices vary to the extreme, in most cases, labor contributes about 50 to 60 percent to the cost of installation. This is true of most floor coverings, except wall-to-wall carpeting, which is less labor-intensive to install.

Tile is sold and installed by the square foot, and when the cost of labor is eliminated, it compares favorably with other types of flooring. An excellent grade of tile, along with other necessary materials, will usually cost between $2 to $4 a foot, less in some cases. When we convert square feet to square yards and consider the high end, it works out to about $36 per yard. A good grade of carpet can easily cost that much. And premium grade vinyl linoleum is not far behind. You must also remember that carpet and linoleum are not permanent materials. So when you compare apples to apples, ceramic tile is a winner every time.

The work is not easy. It is not high-tech, but it is somewhat complex. You can do it, however, just take your time and get your information straight before you begin.

Chapter **4**

Floor preparation

*M*any homes built in the past 30 or 40 years are built on concrete slabs (slab-on-grade). If this is the case with your home, you're off to a running start. Your floor preparation will probably consist of removing the existing floor covering and cleaning up the mess. You might have to fill small depressions in order to flatten out your substrate. In extreme cases, you might actually have to level, or float, the floor in order to get it flat or "on plane."

REMOVING EXISTING FLOORING

Other than ceramic tile or marble, the hardest material to remove from a floor is vinyl linoleum. I use a long-handled floor scraper, but if the area is small, you could use a margin trowel or other type of scraper. There's no easy way to do it. There are motorized scrapers available at rental yards that'll do the trick.

I must warn you that, until a couple decades ago, some linoleum backings contained asbestos. If your floor is more than 10-years-old, it would be a good idea to have it checked by a professional before attempting to remove it.

Once the top, or vinyl layer, has been removed, a backing material that seems to be made of paper remains. Most of the backing must be removed, but small patches, 2 to 3 inches, that just won't come up, can be left in place. My thinking is, if it won't come up now, it'll never come up. If the adhesive is not water-soluble, it won't hurt anything if it is left on the floor, and thin set will adhere to it quite well. To check if it's water-soluble, make a puddle of water on the floor (after the surface layer has been scraped off) and let it stand for a few minutes. If the glue loosens or dissolves, it must be completely removed from the floor. Most linoleum adhesives, however, are not water-soluble.

You might also find a white plasterlike material covering the floor under the adhesive. This is an underlayment that was used to fill depressions and flatten the floor when the linoleum was laid. This can also be left in place if it's well bonded to the concrete.

If you currently have ceramic tile or marble on your floor, you've got two choices: leave it in place and go over it with new tile, or remove it with a hammer and chisel or a jack hammer. If the existing tile is well bonded, I usually just go over it with thin set after ensuring that it's clean, i.e., no wax or grease. Ammonia works well for removing wax, and grease can be cleaned up with soap and hot water.

After the tiled surface has been cleaned, it's a good idea to go over it with a thin coat of latex as a "bonder." The latex is wiped on with a sponge and allowed to dry. Thin set would probably bond to the tiles without it, but it doesn't hurt to have a little insurance.

You can tell whether existing tiles are well bonded by tapping on them with a trowel handle or screwdriver. The difference between the ones that are well bonded, or "solid," and those that are loose, or "hollow," will be readily apparent. Remove only the hollow tiles, if any, with a hammer and chisel, and fill the holes with either another piece of tile, thin set, or other masonry filler. A good filler can be made by mixing pure portland cement with latex. Make it like a paste, and make only a small amount; enough to fill the holes. Spread it in the depressions, and rake off the excess with a short straightedge to get the surface even with the surrounding tiles. Don't forget to wash out your bucket.

Having cleaned up the floor, you're about ready to lay out the job and get on to setting tile. For the individual whose floors are not made of concrete but of wood, you, sir or madam, are about to become a "mud man." And I'm sure you're excited. It's not as easy as falling off a log, but you can handle it.

If it turns out that you're a "mud man," you're not alone. Most older homes, and many of the new ones, especially if you live in the northern part of the country, are built with wood subfloors, and certain procedures must be completed before you can install ceramic tile on them. A masonry substrate must be provided for the tiles to be set on.

You also have two choices. You can either build your substrate on top of the existing subfloor, thereby raising the level of the floor 1 to $1^1/2$ inches; or you can haul out your carpenter tools, tear out the floor, and get your mud bed lower. If you can live with the increase in height, I recommend that you select the first option, but we'll discuss both.

The problem with a wood floor is not that it isn't strong enough to support the weight of the tile or that the tiles won't adhere to it, but rather, it's the "give," or deflection, that is caused when people walk across it. If you can feel the floor give, chances are it is not stable enough to support ceramic tile.

The main problem arises in the grout joints between the tiles. As the floor gives under a "live load," the grout joints are compressed near the surface of the tile and stretched near the bottom. After being under this stress for a period of time, the grout begins to crack, and eventually, chunks of it come out. The result is annoying and unsightly, even though the tiles might still be firmly bonded in place. There is no way to remedy this other than to somehow shore up the substrate or tear out the installation and do it over using some other technique.

I'm not saying tile can't be installed directly over a wood floor, I'm saying I don't do it. Mixing latex or other additives with grout to give it a higher degree of elasticity won't do the job either. Grout, whether it contains latex or not, is basically cement mortar—concrete without the gravel, and it simply won't give enough.

When discussing floors and substrates with people in the trade, you'll hear an array of opinions: "High-tech adhesives and grouts make wood substrates feasible," etc. You'll hear about cement backer board and various other underlayments. But when you ask about lath and mortar, the answer usually goes something like this: "Well, of course, mud is always the best, but it's labor-intensive, and it's messy."

It is my opinion, based on years of experience, that ceramic tile floors should always be installed over a masonry substrate. Tile is expensive, and it's more or less permanent depending on how it's installed. The extra effort expended in doing the job the right way more than pays for itself in the long run.

BUILT-UP METHOD

The easiest—not necessarily the best—way to build a masonry floor is to float the mortar on top of the existing wood floor. You must first consider exterior doors, however, because their thresholds might have to be raised so that doors clear the new floor. Also, you have to give some thought to how the transition from one floor covering to another is to be made, i.e., tile to carpeting, tile to linoleum, etc. Remember, your finished floor will be an inch or so higher than it is now.

In the kitchen, built-in appliances might not clear the new floor should they have to be removed for service or replacement. There is really no good solution for this other than raising the countertops or waiting until there's a problem and tearing out a portion of the floor to get the appliance out. Or, you might consider the other method.

THE OTHER METHOD

If the extra height inherent in building up the floor won't do, you have the option of removing the subfloor and building a lower masonry substrate. It is more labor-intensive and requires a considerable amount of rough carpentry. The idea is to remove the floorboards and reinstall them between the floor joists, thereby lowering the floor the thickness of the floorboards—at least 3/4 of an inch or more (FIG. 2-1).

The best tool to use for the job is a large, industrial reciprocating saw. No other tool will cut against baseboards and cabinet bases as good as this. It's still a chore, but the right type of saw makes it easier.

Once the floorboards have been removed, cleats are nailed securely to the sides of the joists. These will support the floorboards, which are

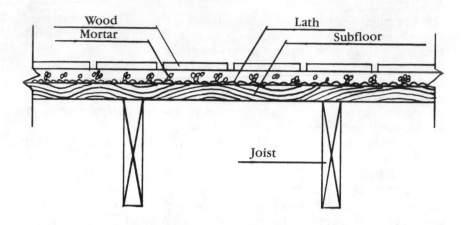

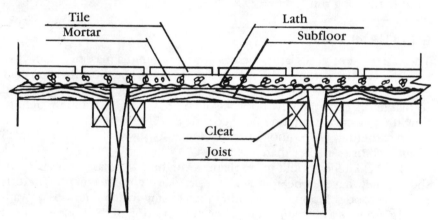

2-1 The "Built-Up Method" (above). The mud bed is floated above the existing floorboards. "The Other Method" (below). The floor boards are cut and reinstalled between the joists.

then cut to fit between the joists. If, for example, the floorboards are 3/4 inch thick, you would nail the cleats to the sides of the joists at least 3/4 inch down from their top edges. The subfloor doesn't have to be perfectly flat, so a little extra depth won't hurt. You can now nail pieces of flooring to the cleats. Make sure everything is well nailed and solid.

The obvious advantage of this method is that you can float your mud bed flush with the adjacent floor, thus raising the finished floor only to the thickness of the tiles themselves. Or, by nailing the floorboards a little lower, you can come up with a tile floor that is on the same level as surrounding floors (FIG. 2-2). You're now ready to begin the mud work. Hang up your carpenter's hat, you're a tile setter again. Except, that is, if you are going to set tile on a bathroom floor. In this case, you still have a few things to do.

Bathroom floors are treated like other floors except that the toilet must be removed. It will be reinstalled after the project is completed. If you're using the built-up method, you might have to use two bowl seals when you reset it, depending on how high the drain flange is above the subfloor. Also, you'll need new bolts—the old ones won't be long enough. If you have a pedestal sink, it will obviously have to be removed. The same goes for bidets, which can be a little tricky to reset. I'll leave advice on that to the plumbers.

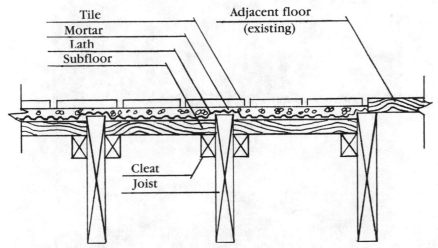

2-2 By nailing the cleats lower, the tile floor can be at the same level as the adjacent floor.

THE MUD WORK
Moisture barrier

Because wood is absorbent, it draws the water out of mortar before it has a chance to cure, so you must protect the mortar from the wood. This is done by covering the area to be tiled with plastic sheeting (poly) or 15-pound felt (tar paper). The material is merely laid on the floor, overlapping the joints a couple of inches. This moisture barrier also helps to prevent moisture from coming up through the tile in the form of condensation. Of course, if your floor is currently covered with vinyl linoleum, you won't need any additional moisture-proofing.

Metal lath

In order to strengthen mortar, or reinforce it so it'll be rigid, as well as keeping it from breaking up under the stress of deflection, you must install metal lath on the floor before floating mud. Expanded metal lath is sold at tile and masonry supply stores. It comes in sheets measuring 26 inches by 8 feet.

When installed, it is overlapped about 2 inches, giving an effective coverage of 16 square feet per sheet. It can be nailed down with roofing or drywall nails or stapled. The fasteners should be about 6 inches apart in both directions. Galvanized chicken wire (poultry netting) can also be used; it works just as well (FIG. 2-3).

Whether lath or chicken wire is used, when it's properly installed with overlapping joints, the end result is called an *armature*; without it, the substrate would crumble and fall apart.

2-3 Nailing down lath using linoleum as a moisture barrier.

Mixing mortar

Because you will be setting tile on the floor and the mud doesn't have to cling to a wall defying gravity, you'll use a mixture called *floor mud* or *deck mud*, which contains no lime. The formula for deck mud is always the same. It is five parts masonry sand to one part portland cement, (5:1). The amount of water added depends on whether the sand is wet or dry.

Portland cement is sold in 94-pound sacks at masonry and tile supplies. It's also available at lumberyards and home centers. Masonry sand can be purchased at topsoil yards, landscaping supply stores, and from masonry suppliers. Don't use the prepared mortar sold at home centers. It contains lime, which will make it harder to use. It is also expensive. It takes too many of those little sacks to make the amount of mud that can be made from a pile of sand and a sack of portland cement.

The easiest way to mix floor mud is to pile the sand on a driveway or other concrete slab and measure it by the shovel-full. Load the appropriate amount of cement on top of the sand and then count the shovelfuls to achieve the proper ratio of sand and cement—5:1. Now, toss it or turn it over with the shovel until the sand is completely coated with cement. When it is thoroughly mixed, it's time to add the water (FIGS. 2-4 through 2-7).

2-4 Dry-mixing the mortar.

Imagine yourself at the beach making a sand castle. The proper consistency for sand castles contains just enough water to hold the particles together when molding. If there's too much, the sand will slump. If there's too little, the sand won't hold together. This is the consistency you're looking for. Your mortar should be just like the sand at the beach—with one exception—if you were to make a sand castle out of it, it would become a permanent fixture in your driveway.

Take it easy on the water. Add small amounts at a time, and keep tossing the mix with the shovel. When it resembles beach sand, except in color, and you can mold it with your hands, it's ready to use. Load it into a couple of buckets and carry it to the work site.

2-5 Don't overdo it with the water.

2-6 Blending in the water.

2-7 Tossing and turning.

Floor mud can also be mixed in a mixing box or wheelbarrow. The process is the same only it's easier to use a hoe than a shovel. A masonry hoe is nice but a garden hoe will do the job. When mixing with a hoe, chop down at the mud, reaching all the way to the bottom of the box or wheelbarrow. This chopping motion pulls the mix from one end of the box to the other. Continue chopping until you have that sand castle consistency. Remember to dry-mix the mud before adding the water, and add just enough water to moisten the sand so that the particles cling together.

At this point, you're ready to build, or "float," the floor. If you still have mud piled in your driveway or your wheelbarrow, cover it with something to prevent it from drying out. A piece of plastic sheeting or anything that will prevent moisture from escaping will do. Depending on weather conditions, mortar will be good for about an hour to an hour and a half. After that, or when the mud begins to dry on the surface, it should be discarded. It won't reach what is referred to as "peak strength" when cured.

BUILDING SCREEDS

If you were to just dump the mud on the floor and start spreading it around, chances are you would accomplish nothing more than making a mess. In order to come up with a floor that is flat and level, you must have something to work toward. Screeds are built from mortar and ultimately become a part of the floated floor. Pathways of mud are formed at the edges of the floor, which are then compacted with a flat trowel and leveled off at the height of the proposed finished floor. You might also need additional intermediate screeds depending on the width of the area you intend to float. As the areas between the screeds are floated, you draw the straightedge (wood board) between the screeds, being careful not to damage the mud screeds with the ends of the straightedge (FIG. 2-8).

2-8 Building screeds.

Generally, screeds should be roughly parallel to each other, no more than about 5 feet apart. There is a limit to the length of a straightedge that can be easily handled by one person. A professional can usually manage an 8-foot straightedge with comfort, but a novice might be more at ease with a 4- or 5-foot-long straightedge. You've got to be able to keep an eye on both ends of the straightedge to ensure that you don't dig into screeds, thereby making your floor uneven.

Before you start building screeds, it's necessary to know the highest point in the subfloor. The minimum thickness of a floated floor over a wood subfloor is about 3/4 of an inch with 5/8 of an inch bridging over small areas. If you think floors are normally level, Think again. A level subfloor is the exception to the rule.

So, holding your level on top of the longest straightedge you have, move around the floor to determine the highest point. This will be the point from which the floor will be started. Make a small mound of mortar, about one foot in diameter, at the highest point, and tamp it down with a flat trowel. The mound should be basically flat on top—its surface should be about an inch above the subfloor.

With the edge of your level, scrape the top surface of the mound down to about ⅝ of an inch, keeping your eye on the bubble. The top of the mound must be level in all directions, so change the direction of the level once or twice. After you've leveled the mound at about ⅝ of an inch above the subfloor, you're ready to begin building the screeds (FIGS. 2-9 and 2-10). If the floor is to be built level, this will be be your starting point—your reference point as you go along.

2-9 Building the reference point.

In most cases, you can build a floor level, but if your subfloor is way out of level, you might want to float the floor slightly out of level so that it doesn't end up 2 inches higher than an adjacent floor. In this case, a long straightedge is used to build the screeds instead of the level, but for now, let's try to level the floor.

You're going to build screeds with the edge of a 4-foot level or with a shorter level held on top of a 4- or 5-foot straightedge. Obviously, it'll be easier to use a 4-foot level. Begin by dumping mortar along an edge of the

2-10 Leveling the reference point in all directions.

floor. It might be along a wall, a cabinet base, or in the open. If you're working out in the open, and using the built-up method, let the mud go past the edge of the lath an inch or so. It can be trimmed off straight later. If you're using the "other" method, your substrate will be screeded even with the adjacent floor.

You need a path of mud about 6 to 8 inches wide running along the edge of the floor—just dump it and spread it with the trowel. Now, tamp (compact) the surface with a flat trowel. Your path of mortar should be 1 to 1½-inch high. You don't have to tamp hard on the mud. Just get it well compacted.

The next step is to wear down the mortar at any point on the screed to the height of the original reference point—the little mound of mud you built and leveled. There are several ways this can be done. You can bridge across from the reference point to the screed with the level, if it'll reach, or you can use the level in conjunction with a longer straightedge. You could also build another reference point between the original mound and the screed. The idea is to arrive at a point on the screed that is at the same level (height) as the reference point (FIG. 2-11).

Holding the level along the length of the screed, begin moving it back and forth, keeping your eye on the bubble to wear the top of the screed down to the level point (FIG. 2-12). Once you've got a section of the screed level with the original reference point, it's simply a matter of mov-

2-11 Get any point on the screed level with the reference point.

2-12 Leveling the screed.

ing the level along the screed and repeating the wearing down process until the screed is level along it's entire length. When a section has been leveled, lightly smooth the surface with the flat trowel, just enough to smooth the grains of sand. Don't push down too hard, you might put a dip in the screed.

You'll need a screed about 4 or 5 feet from the first one and roughly parallel to it. You can bridge across with the level from the mud just leveled or you can return to your original reference point. It doesn't matter which way you do it, but it is a good idea to occasionally return to the original point to check yourself (FIG. 2-13).

2-13 Checking the height of a screed.

When leveling mud against a wall or a cabinet base, cut the excess mortar (the mud pushed against the wall) even using the flat trowel. Make a clean line along the vertical surface, be it a baseboard, cabinet base, or a wall (FIG. 2-14).

Once you've got two screeds running parallel to each other, you can begin filling in between them with mud and float a section of floor, or you could build more screeds. If your floor is going to be built exactly level, it doesn't matter. You can build additional screeds as you need them. On the other hand, if you've decided that the subfloor is so far out of level as to make it impractical to float the substrate level, you'll have to change techniques. See "Floating a floor out of level" in the next section.

2-14 Cleaning up the screed.

FLOATING A FLOOR

To float a floor, begin in the area farthest from your mortar supply. You don't want to work yourself into a corner you can't get out of. I know it sounds stupid, but if you're not thinking about it, it can happen—it has happened to me on more than one occasion.

Filling mud between screeds is easy. Fill only an area you can reach comfortably—2 feet or so. Otherwise, you'll have to kneel in the mud to work on it. Fill the area with mud and push it around with the trowel until it's about a 1/2 inch above the tops of the screeds. Now, tamp it down with the flat trowel.

With the straightedge held on edge, begin scraping the mortar down to the level of the screeds, being careful not to dig into the screeds themselves. Start at the point farthest away from your knees and rake the mud back towards you with small strokes (FIGS. 2-15 and 2-16).

As the excess mud builds up in front of the straightedge, scoop it out of the way with the flat trowel and continue scraping until you've got the mortar down to the level of the screeds. If there are voids, fill them with more mud, tamp them down, and scrape them off with the straightedge.

When the area is filled and leveled, smooth the surface lightly with the flat trowel as you did when you were building the screeds (FIG. 2-17). If there is mud built up along a wall, cut it clean with the blade of the trowel.

2-15 Using the straightedge.

2-16 Don't push down too hard.

2-17 Smoothing the surface.

When you've completed one area, move back another couple of feet and repeat the process (FIG. 2-18). Just keep going until you run out of screeds or until you run out of mud. If you still have mortar and you need more screeds, build them. If you run out of mud, you've got a couple of choices. You can mix more mud immediately, or you can stand around a while and think about it. But don't stand around until you've washed your tools.

Standing around

The best way to stand around is to spread your feet about 26 inches apart, fold your arms in front of you, and assume a facial expression that is both contemplative and, at the same time, authoritative. Rocking back and forth on your heels and toes doesn't hurt. If you remain in this position for more than a minute, it's a good idea to turn your head from side to side while muttering to yourself. The cardinal rule is—never take your eyes off the work; make it seem as difficult as possible.

Floating a floor out of level

Floating a floor out of level? I'm sure there will be some raised eyebrows over this one, but occasionally, there's no other way to go. Many older

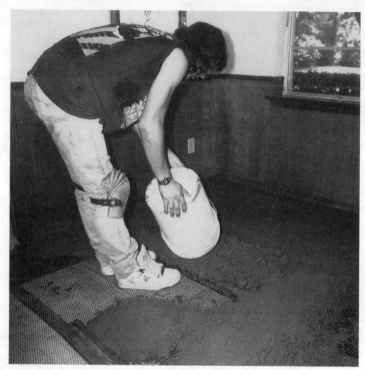

2-18 Beginning the next "pull."

homes, and some new ones, have floors that aren't anywhere near level, and if it's necessary to meet an adjacent floor area, it makes sense to more or less follow the subfloor when floating. Think of it this way; you've lived with the floor out of level, why not continue to do so. You won't notice the difference.

Floating a floor out of level involves a technique using a long straight-edge—8 or 10 feet—instead of a level to scrape off the tops of the screeds. You make two mounds of mud, 8 or 10 feet apart, get them about 3/4 of an inch high, and build the screed between the two. Unless the floor is out of level in all directions, you'll be able to use the level in some segments.

Your finished floor will definitely not be level. It must, however, be built "on plane," or flat. There cannot be up's and down's—no ski chutes. I'm certain you won't find this technique listed in any tile setter's manuals, and it should only be considered as a last resort.

Anyway, let's get back to floating a level floor. If it has taken you a while to build two or three screeds, and you still have mud mixed, perhaps you should begin floating the area between two of the screeds. Remember, your mud isn't going to be usable after an hour to an hour and a half.

Floating behind doors

Here, floating behind doors is specifically referring to entry doors and other exterior doors. Generally, you'll want to float the area behind the door, and at the same time, work your way out of it. Otherwise, you might have to track through the house and over the carpet, possibly incurring the wrath of your partner.

The doors in most entryways open "in," and most of them open against a wall, so you'll have to close the door to float behind it. The best time to float the area behind the door is when you're building the screed that runs along the wall the door opens against. Just make the screed wider than normal so that you have about 6 inches protruding under the door when it is open. You can bridge across from another screed and float the area level, smooth the surface with the trowel, and open the door. You can then float the area farthest from the door and back your way out (FIG. 2-19).

When you've finished, lock the door to protect your work. Hopefully, you've left another door unlocked so that you can get back into the house and sit around for a while. Don't sit around until you've figured out how to clean up the mess in the driveway, though.

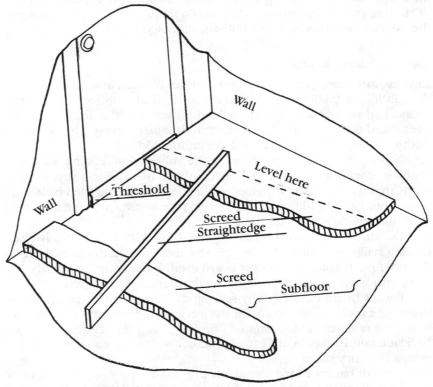

2-19 Floating behind a door.

After you've carefully cleaned all your tools, including the straight-edges and buckets, you can clean the driveway by scraping up the excess mortar with your shovel and disposing of it. Hose the driveway off. You can swish a broom around to dislodge the mortar that is stuck to the concrete and hose it again. You'll probably end up leaving a little cement residue, but it's only cement on a cement driveway, and besides, it might camouflage some of the oil spots that have accumulated over the years. After you've done all of this, you can spend the rest of the day sitting around admiring your handiwork because it must "set" overnight so that you can get on it to set the tile.

Sitting around

Sitting around is an art that might require some instruction. Find a comfortable spot that affords you a sideways view of your project, but don't be too obvious about it. You can appear to be watching television or reading a book while casting an occasional glance in the direction of your handiwork when nobody's looking. You've already demonstrated how technically difficult the job was during the "Standing around" stage. Now, you must give the impression that it was, for you, a routine chore of no consequence. Under no circumstance should you get caught in the "Standing around" position, as this would be bad form, and it might give the impression that you're not entirely sure of yourself.

Cement backer board

In some instances, cement backer board can be used instead of mortar if the subfloor is totally supported underneath. If the subfloor is extremely sound and relatively free from deflection, you could nail backer board over it and install the tile directly onto it. It must, however, be noted that nothing is as good as the lath and mortar method.

You might consider shoring up the subfloor by adding additional joists or other bracing. And, although I seldom use backer board, it seems to me that if it were actually glued to the floorboards and then nailed, the floor would gain rigidity. Of course, gluing the material down makes it difficult to provide a moisture barrier.

Cement backer board is nailed to the floor with $1^1/2$-inch galvanized roofing nails—the more, the better. The moisture barrier is laid on the floor before installing the backer board itself. If the floor is currently covered with vinyl linoleum, the moisture barrier can be omitted.

Backer board can be cut by scoring the face side with an old screwdriver or a tool specially made for the job and sold where backer board is sold. The material is then bent or "broken," and the reinforcing on the backside cut. Backer board can also be cut with a circular saw equipped with a masonry blade.

Cement backer board is available in 3-×-5-foot sheets, $1/2$ inch thick. It is also manufactured in 4-×-8-foot sheets, but these are not usually stocked and must be special ordered.

Floating concrete floors

Because of its water content, concrete is extremely difficult to work with, and the floors in houses built with the "slab-on-grade" technique are never completely flat. Most floors, however, are poured level enough to allow ceramic tiles to be set directly over them, but occasionally, the slabs are out of level far enough to justify floating them with mortar.

The technique for floating concrete floors is the same as that used for wood floors except that mortar is bonded directly to the slab and lath is not used. The concrete is prepared with cement slurry, which is used as a bonding agent.

Because concrete can totally support mortar, floated mud can be applied thinner than that which is applied to a wood floor—a layer of about 3/8 of an inch or so should be sufficient. The mortar does not have to have the mass it does on a wood floor because there is no deflection.

When portland cement slurry is used, it is applied over small areas, and the mortar must come in contact with it before it dries. A couple of minutes or so at the most. Cement slurry is made by placing 2 or 3 inches of water in the bottom of a bucket and adding cement. The mix is watery, and the slurry is more or less slopped onto the floor and spread around with a broom. Just remember that mortar must be spread over it immediately.

Another method of bonding is to wet the concrete liberally and then sprinkle pure cement over it. What you end up with is slurry. You must still cover the area with mud before the bonding material dries.

Screeds are built, and the floor is then floated. The next day, before any layout work is done, it's necessary to tap on the entire surface of the floor to check for "hollow" spots. A broom handle makes a good tapper, or the handle of a margin trowel will work. If a hollow area is discovered, it must be removed and redone. Beat it out with a hammer then re-float it with mortar, or fill it with latex mixed with pure cement. The reasoning is simple. Mortar floated over a concrete slab is not reinforced, and if not bonded to the slab, it has very little strength.

Expansion joints

In larger homes built with the "slab-on-grade" method, joints are sometimes placed in the slab to allow for expansion and contraction of the concrete with temperature change. These joints cannot be ignored when ceramic tile is installed. The joints are usually located directly under walls and partitions, and continue through doorways. If your tile floor must cross an expansion joint, provision must be made for it.

When floating mortar across an expansion joint, cut out a 1/4-inch-wide groove directly above the joint. Likewise, when installing the tile, try to arrange a grout joint so that it falls directly above it. If this is not possible, the tiles crossing the expansion joint must be cut directly above it, allowing for a 1/8- to 1/4-inch gap. Finally, the joint is filled not with grout, but with a more elastic material—caulking. Grout manufacturers usually produce caulking in the colors of their most popular grouts. Special expansion joint material, which can be tinted with color, is available through most tile suppliers.

Control joints

Control joints are sometimes placed under partitions and walls. They appear as cracks running across doorways. Control joints must be treated as expansion joints.

In my area, control joints are seldom used, and the result is cracked floors in most houses. These cracks usually occur during construction as the concrete cures and cause no problem. I go over them, making sure the customer is aware of them. If the floor should shift or settle in the future, the tiles set above the crack will probably develop hairline cracks. What can be done? Nothing. Any repairs made to existing concrete slabs are little more than cosmetic. They don't cure the problem, so I don't lose any sleep over them. Still, I must make you aware of the possibilities.

Chapter 5

Floor layout

*O*nce the floor has been prepared with con-
crete, mortar, or cement backer board, it's time to lay out the project and
begin setting tile. There is always more than one way to lay out a floor—
the size and placement of the cuts, the direction of the grout lines, centering, the tile pattern, etc.—all have a bearing on how the floor is laid out,
but there is usually only one "best" way to do the job.

In an entryway that is basically a rectangle, for example, the cuts
going along both walls, as viewed from the doorway, should be approximately the same size. It wouldn't do to have the cuts 6 inches on one side
and 3 on the other. Generally, the "field," or area of tile to be installed,
should be shifted so that the largest possible cuts can be used and tile
appears balanced.

If, for example, you were to lay a row of tiles across an entryway,
allowing for the proper spacing of grout joints, and discovered that the
cuts along the walls were going to be less than half of a tile, you would
need to shift the field to one side so that the cuts are larger than half a tile.
This is called *centering*, and it is covered thoroughly in this chapter.

CENTERING THE FLOOR

If you draw a "reference line" down the center of any tiled floor, you'll
discover one of two things: that the center tile is astride the centerline or
there are tiles on either side of the line. Therefore, when you lay out your
tile, you are either going to have a center tile or there'll be a grout joint
running down the center of the floor. Whichever arrangement allows for
the largest cuts at the sides is the correct one (FIG. 2-20).

If your floor has offsets or is in the shape of an L, for example, there
are other considerations. The field must be shifted in the other direction
to allow for reasonable cuts at the sides of the L. This can all be done with
a measuring tape, but it's a good idea to actually lay out pieces of tile in all
directions to ensure that the cuts are going to work out well.

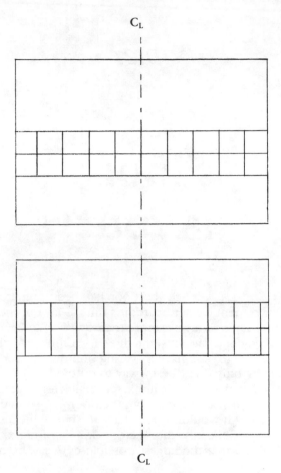

2-20 There are two ways of centering. Don't end up with the "skinnies."

If the area to be tiled abuts carpeting or other flooring along a good portion of its edge, the tiles along that edge should be full pieces if possible. The tiles along the opposite wall would then be cut to fit, provided the cuts are reasonable in size and not unsightly. Only if this is not possible, should the tiles along the open edge be cut, and then just enough to allow for more pleasing cuts at the wall (FIG. 2-21).

I don't give much consideration to cuts that will be made in closets. It is more important to center the area that will be seen. Workmanship in closets, however, should be of the same quality as that in visible areas of the floor.

Kitchens and baths

In a kitchen, it is not generally feasible to center the field of tile. One side of the kitchen usually contains a row of cabinets and spaces for the refrig-

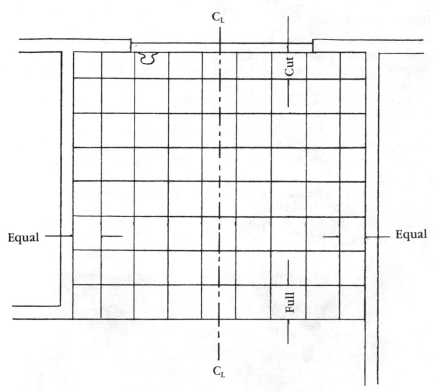

2-21 Layout at open edge of floor.

erator and stove, perhaps even an island. Most kitchens are not a single rectangle, but a series of them, all of which must be considered when laying out the floor. It is just not possible to center the field because there are too many small fields involved.

The same type of centering problems occur in most small bathrooms. Although most are basic rectangles, the space taken up by the vanity cabinet results in an L-shape floor.

The best thing to do is to experiment with the layout until the cuts at all extremities of the floor are reasonable and not unsightly. Under no circumstance should there be ''skinny'' cuts in easily seen areas. If necessary, place them under cabinet toe spaces or behind the refrigerator or other appliances. The area of floor that is first seen as you walk into the room should be considered first and foremost. It is then a matter of shifting the field slightly so that cuts in other areas appear reasonable.

Almost every do-it-yourself article I've read on laying floors advises to find the exact center of the floor and begin laying out from that point, working in all directions. This is fine if the floor happens to be a nice clean rectangle or square. Take a look around and you'll find that this is seldom the case. In my house, it occurs in just two rooms—the bedrooms—the least likely of places to install a ceramic tile floor. Carpeting is much warmer on the tootsies when you climb out of bed in the morning.

Raised entryways

In some homes, the entry area has been raised above the level of the adjacent floor, which is usually tiled along with the rest of the entry. This step is referred to as a *riser*, and it has a definite effect on the layout of the entryway.

Tiles installed on the edge of the entry immediately above the riser are almost always uncut pieces that protrude over the edge of the floor and overlap tiles that are later installed vertically on the riser itself. In a very few instances, bullnose pieces are available that match the field tiles, but this is not usually the case. The field tiles themselves will form their own edge.

What all this means is simply that you must begin the layout at the riser, allowing for the necessary overhang. The cuts, whatever size or shape, will be made at the opposite edge of the floor. Figure 2-22 demonstrates the technique.

2-22 Tiles above risers are full pieces.

SQUARING THE FLOOR

It is essential to square the floor. You cannot assume that walls have been built at right angles to each other, because this is not usually the case. Although ceramic tiles, because of the methods used to produce them, are not without flaws, they are, for the most part, square. And the layout must be square or the tiles simply won't fit in.

To square the floor, measure off two equal points at the longest wall bordering your floor so you can make a line parallel to that wall. Place a pencil mark at both of these points. Pulling the line of the chalk box taut between the two points, snap a line on the floor. The position of the line is not important, but position it so that it'll clear cabinets and other obstructions when extended across the floor. You'll need another line that intersects the first at a 90-degree angle. In other words, it'll be perpendicular to the first line. The best way to do this is to use the three-four-five method (FIGS. 2-23 to 2-27).

2-23 Establishing one side of the right triangle on the reference line.

The three-four-five method

Without getting into the finer points of plane geometry, the three-four-five method enables you to construct a triangle with one of its angles equal to 90 degrees. This is called a *right triangle*, and for our purposes, if one of its sides measures 3 feet and another 4 feet, the third side will always measure 5 feet. And multiples of three, four, and five can be used; for example, six, eight, and ten.

2-24 Tracing an arc with the measuring tape.

2-25 Establishing the perpendicular point.

2-26 Snapping the perpendicular line.

2-27 We snapped the third side of the triangle for illustration. This is not normally done.

If you mark a point anyplace on the reference line and another 4 feet away from the first, you've established one side of the right triangle (FIG. 2-23). Using the measuring tape as a compass, carefully trace an arc, 3 feet away from the first point, which is approximately perpendicular to that point (FIG. 2-24). From the other point, measure, roughly diagonally, a distance of 5 feet, and trace another arc to intersect with the first arc you drew (FIG. 2-25). The point where the two arcs intersect is perpendicular to the first point on the line. Now snap a line through the intersection of the arcs and through the first point on the line with a chalk box. The second line is perpendicular to the first (FIG. 2-26).

The lines have nothing to do with the placement of tiles, but every subsequent line will be parallel to one or the other of the "reference lines." This is called *squaring the floor*.

You can also square a floor using a steel square. Hold one leg of the square along the first reference line and draw the perpendicular line along the other leg with a pencil. Unless the floor area to be tiled is very small, however, this method is not accurate enough, and it's a good idea to master the three-four-five method. A square will do the job on a floor that is four or five feet wide, if used carefully.

CENTERING THE TILES

When an entryway abuts the walls on both sides, looking through the doorway, it is called a closed entry and, as I mentioned earlier in the chapter, you'll want the tiles to be centered. Again, you'll either have a center tile or a centerline. If, after having positioned a row of tiles across your entry, you determine that there are going to be full tiles on both sides of the line, you should offset the centerline by half of a grout joint in order to end up with equal cuts on both sides of the floor.

When you begin setting tile, one row of tiles will be set "on" the line, and the next row will be set "off" the line, or one grout space away (see FIG. 2-28). If the centerline were truly "dead center," the field would be shifted slightly to one side and the cuts at the walls would not be equal from one side of the floor to the other. If the cuts at the walls are to be of equal size and the joints are to be $1/4$ inch, which is normal for floor tiles, you'll move the line $1/8$ of an inch to either side.

So, if you're going to have full tiles on either side of the centerline, measure across the floor and divide by two. Then, from the longest wall, measure to the center and add $1/8$ of an inch. Make a pencil mark at this point. Transfer the measurement to both ends of the floor by measuring from the longest wall and marking the points with a pencil. Snap a line through the points, and you'll have your "off center" centerline. The line has now become a layout line, meaning a row of tiles will be set with their edges along it and all subsequent lines will either be parallel or perpendicular to this line.

If, on the other hand, you've positioned a row of tiles across your floor and determined that you're going to have a center tile, simply center a piece of tile using your measuring tape. Once you've done this, make a

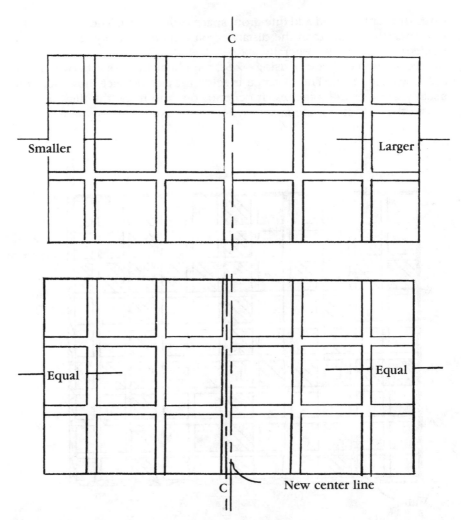

2-28 In the field (above), we've used the centerline as a layout line and set a row of tiles along it. Thus, the field is offset by one grout space, making the cuts at the edge unequal. By offsetting the centerline (below) by half a grout space and setting a row of tiles along it, we've equalized the cuts at both edges.

mark at one of its edges. Now, by measuring the distance from the mark to the longest wall, transfer the mark to points near each end of the floor and snap a line through them. You now have your first layout line, along which a row of tiles will be set.

Layout lines

To determine how far apart your layout lines should be, lay a row of several tiles along any line, allowing for desired grout joints. Measure across three or four tiles, and add one grout space to your total. The lines should not be farther apart than the distance you can comfortably reach across while on your knees, generally about 2 feet.

For example, if you're using 8 × 8s, there'll be three tiles between layout lines (FIG. 2-29). The distance is seldom exactly 2 feet, however, it's usually 24¼ or 24½ inches. It depends on who made the tiles, and in most other countries, the metric system of measure is used.

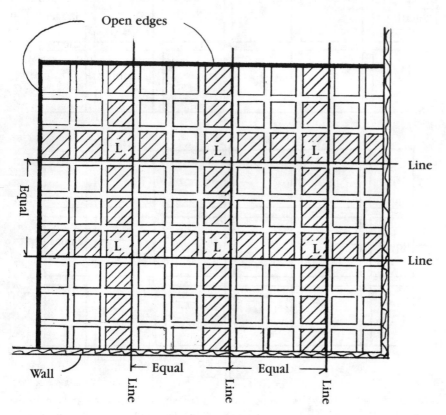

2-29 In the grid system, the shaded tiles are set on the lines and the unshaded tiles are set off the lines. Lead tiles (L) are set first and all other tiles are set off them.

Grout joints

The width of grout joints is a matter of taste, but the normal spacing for ceramic floor tiles has for years been about a ¼ inch, and that's what people are accustomed to seeing.

In the case of Saltillo and terra-cotta tiles, which are very irregular in size and shape, the spacing must be wider—about a half inch. If you try to set them closer together, you might find that suddenly the tiles won't fit in the space you've provided! Still, no floor tile is perfect and some are calibrated better than others, so don't try to set them too close together.

The next step is to lay out the floor in the other direction. As we've discussed, the tiles installed along the "open" edge of the floor, lengthy areas bordering carpeting or other floor covering, should be left uncut. Begin by laying a row of several tiles along the layout line, starting with a full piece at the open edge of the floor. Now, measure across three or four tiles, depending on their size, and determine how far apart the layout lines must be. Don't forget to add the extra grout space (FIG. 2-29).

By "stepping off" the distance with a measuring tape to the opposite edge of the floor, you can determine the size of the cuts at that edge. Or, if you're not really that proud of your measuring capabilities, you can lay the row of tiles all the way to the edge and then determine how the cuts will look. If the cuts are going to be reasonable in size, you're ready to put down all your layout lines.

If the cuts are not going to be presentable, you must consider cutting off the tiles at the open edge and shifting the field in that direction. Cut off only enough to make the cuts at the other edge look decent. You should still have almost a whole tile at the open edge. The exception to the rule occurs when using patterned tiles or tiles containing printed borders. Tiles of this type should always be left full at open edges. You must live with the cuts or choose another tile.

Generally, open edges refer to lengthy edges of the floor that are highly noticeable when one enters a room. This does not include the areas inside standard doorways. Cuts generally appear in these areas, and they're not unsightly unless they're skinny. If there are no open edges, it's simply a matter of arranging the field so that the cuts at all edges are presentable, as was discussed earlier.

If possible, you should make your first perpendicular line at a point where it will become an actual layout line. You can do this by measuring along the established line to a point where the grout lines of the field will intersect. Then employ the three-four-five method to establish your perpendicular line at this point. It is then simply a matter of establishing the remaining layout lines from this intersection. If you're going to have a cut at the edge of the floor, figure the cut, plus two or three full tiles, and the grout joints. Make your mark, and snap the line across the reference line at that point, employing the three-four-five method.

The grid system

Throughout the years, I've seen all types of layout systems designed for keeping the courses of tile straight and square. But I've found the best to be what I call the "grid system." It is almost foolproof and entails laying out the entire floor before beginning to set the tiles. The main advantage is that you'll know the size and placement of all cuts and how they will look before the first piece of tile is installed. Have you heard this before?

Plastic joint spacers are available from tile suppliers. I use them on vertical surfaces to keep the tiles from sliding down. I never use them on floors, and you shouldn't either. Tiles are not perfect, as I said, and using spacers will only cause problems. A variation of only $1/32$ of an inch will throw you out of whack in two or three courses. Lay out the lines using the grid system and stay with them.

From your perpendicular reference lines, which should by now be layout lines, measure and mark a series of points along opposite sides of the floor. The distance between the marks will, of course, be the space that three or four tiles take plus the width of one grout space. All distances should be equal (FIG. 2-29). Now, snap the lines across the floor between the points, and you've got all your layout lines in one direction. Repeat the process in the other direction, and the entire floor has been laid out (FIG. 2-30). Any mistakes you might have made in figuring the size of cuts will be apparent because you'll have lines running in close proximity to all walls and cabinets. After surveying the entire layout and checking it with the measuring tape, you're ready to set tile . . . unless you want to lay the tiles diagonally to the walls. Or, what if the tiles aren't square? What if they are oblong or hexagons?

Before we get going, let's discuss some of the "tricky" layout options that are possible. The square layout is the most popular because it is uncluttered and doesn't detract from other room design elements.

2-30 Snapping layout lines.

FLOOR LAYOUT OPTIONS

There are many ways a tile floor can be arranged. The square pattern is the most common (and the most popular, I should say) because it is not cluttered. It doesn't distract from other elements of a room's decor, such as wall coverings, drapes, and furniture. It is appealing without being "busy." But after all is said and done, layout remains a matter of personal preference.

Patterned floor tiles

Proper layout is the most important element in installing tile floors. It's often a case of trial and error. Therefore, it is crucial to make those errors and correct them before the first piece of material is installed, especially if the tiles are patterned.

Flowers and other patterns should face in the same direction, which is really not a problem, but layout really gets tricky when it takes four tiles to complete one element of a pattern. In this case, you must not only be concerned with centering individual tiles, but with centering four at a time. The best way to do this is to arrange the tiles on the floor until you get them the way you want them. This is my trade secret, and it's foolproof.

Diagonal patterns

In small rooms, and some larger ones, laying the tile at a 45-degree angle to the walls visually "pushes" the walls out and causes the room to appear larger. The grout lines are longer than if they were running straight across the room. A surrounding square border of tile is also a design possibility.

When laying out a diagonal pattern, the principles of the square layout are employed. After the floor has been squared, it is necessary to turn the reference lines 45 degrees to the walls. This involves bisecting two of the angles formed by the intersecting "square" reference lines. If you're like me, you have forgotten some of your high school geometry. Bisecting angles is explained in FIG. 2-31. When the reference lines are diagonal, it's just a matter of centering the field so that the edge cuts are balanced and eye-appealing. Although this can be done by measuring, it might be better to lay tiles along the diagonal lines and then center them. If a square border is desired, the diagonal cuts, if possible, should be halves, allowing the alternating full tiles to remain uncut.

Brick patterns

When using tiles that are rectangular rather than square, the layout possibilities are endless. The tiles I'm referring to are "modular." In other words, they must, after considering grout spacing, be exactly half as wide as they are long (see FIGS. 2-32 and 2-33). Rectangular tiles are laid out using the same principles as square layout. After squaring the floor, it's merely a

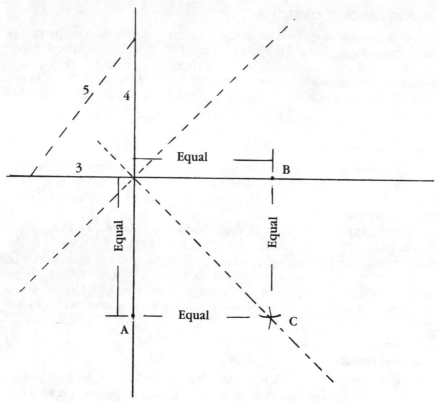

2-31 After using the 3-4-5 method to form perpendicular reference lines, measure from the intersection an equal distance along both lines (Points A and B). Trace arcs whose radii are equal to form Point C and the intersection.

matter of centering. "Soldier Course" borders can also be incorporated into the pattern.

Hexagons and octagons

The basic layout techniques are the same for all floors regardless of the shape of the tiles, including hexagons and octagons. It's a matter of centering the field and arranging the lines so that the tiles can be set along them. When setting irregular-shaped tiles, a straightedge can be used to help keep the courses straight. (See FIGS. 2-34 and 2-35.)

Inlays

When a border is not against a wall or at the edge of a layout, it is called an *inlay* (FIG. 2-32). Often, inlay tiles are a different color or a different size. The main consideration is that the tiles used for the inlay be of the same

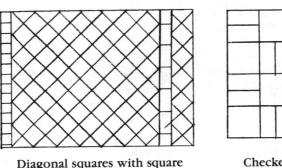

Diagonal squares with square border and inlay.

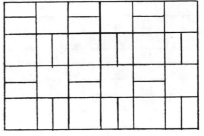

Checkerboard variation using squares and rectangles.

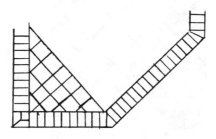

Diagonal squares with soldier course of rectangles.

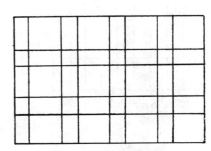

Square grid (formal).

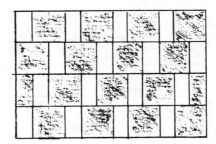

Squares offset by rectangles.

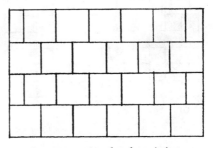

Squares using broken joints.

2-32 These are only a few of the possibilities. Use your imagination.

thickness as the field tiles. If this is not the case, one or the other will have to be built up by buttering thin set onto their backs as they're installed. This is a painstaking process and should be avoided if possible. It's not

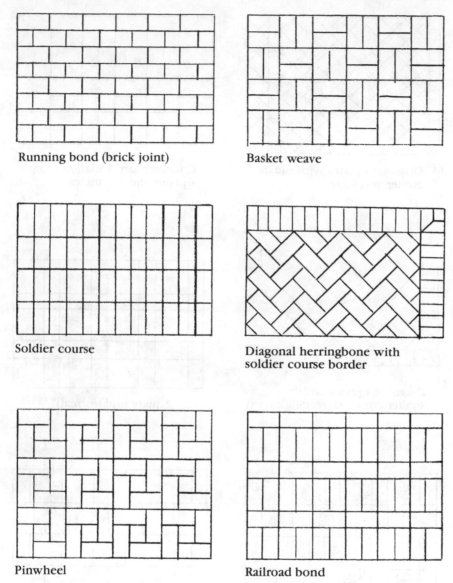

Running bond (brick joint)

Basket weave

Soldier course

Diagonal herringbone with
soldier course border

Pinwheel

Railroad bond

2-33 Using modular rectangles, the possibilities are endless.

bad when the inlay tiles are thinner, however, because there aren't as
many of them to raise. If the inlays are thicker, the entire field must be
raised to their level, and folks, I'm not prepared to try to explain how this
can be done—in a book.

Remember that the layout process is all-important. Don't be tempted
to hurry it, and never try to do the job without it. When laying out tile,
you're drawing a full-scale picture of your project on the floor and if you
follow it, your floor will be picture perfect.

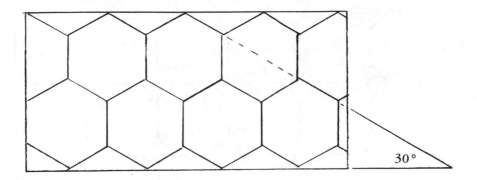

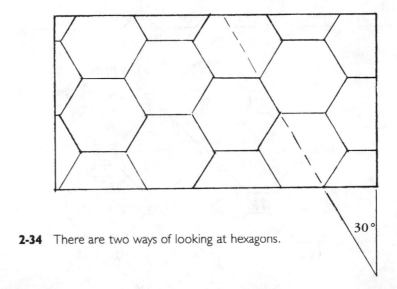

2-34 There are two ways of looking at hexagons.

ESTIMATING MATERIAL

Tile is sold by the square foot, so estimating how much it takes to cover your floor is a matter of converting the area into square feet and adding for waste. If the floor is a basic rectangle, figure the length times the width in feet and add 3 to 4 percent to the total. If the floor is not a rectangle, divide it into smaller rectangles, figure their areas, and add them together. There will be more waste in this case because more cuts will be needed. I usually allow 5 percent for waste when there are a number of offsets. Ideally, you'll have enough tile to make all the cuts and have a few pieces left over for replacements in the future.

During manufacture, tile seldom comes out the same way twice. Variations in shade and calibration are common. Don't expect to return to the store for additional tile that perfectly matches the tile you've already installed. It might be possible, but don't depend on it.

On the other hand, don't overdo it when buying tile. When buying

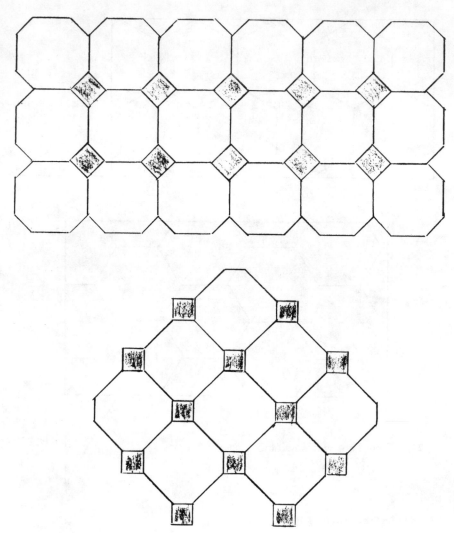

2-35 There are two ways of looking at octagons; it depends on which way you want the "dots" to run.

from a tile supplier, products can be returned, but a restocking charge of 20 to 25 percent is deducted from the refund. Therefore, do your calculations carefully and double check them before buying the tile.

The amount of thin set, grout, and other cement products needed will depend on the type of tile purchased and the nature of your project. The people at the tile supply store can accurately estimate your needs. Cement products are not usually returnable, so don't buy more than you need.

FINISHING UP

In a how-to book, the author is to assume nothing, but I do hope you swept the floor before laying it out, but if you didn't . . . not to worry. In fact, sweeping is a constant process when setting tile on floors. Just moving across the floor on your knees stirs up debris, and bits of tile from the use of the biters accumulate. Sweeping tends to obliterate the layout lines that were so painstakingly established. So, from time to time, the lines will have to be re-snapped. When re-snapping lines, it's always good to go back to the original pencil marks, if possible. Otherwise, make sure you're directly over the original line.

A word about lines

Lines are never wrong, provided you've taken the pains to check them out before you've begun setting the tile. Stay with your lines, and stay within the grid squares. Tiles can vary slightly in size and shape, but the lines are not going to move. Once you've begun, do not stray from the lines!

Chapter **6**

Setting
floor tiles

Once all of the preliminaries have been completed, it is time to set the floor tiles. The rest of the job is relatively easy. The hardest part is over.

GETTING STARTED

The first thing to do before you begin setting tiles is to mix up the ceramic tiles. Because floor tiles are usually varied slightly in color and pattern, you need to blend several boxes so that variations are less conspicuous. If the floor is small, blend all your tiles before starting. If you notice severe variations, however, return the tiles to the supplier before installation.

Spreading thin set

Once you have thoroughly blended up the tiles, you must mix up the thin set. Place 2 to 3 inches of water in the bottom of a bucket, and add the dry thin set. You should be using the gray thin set specially formulated for concrete floors. Stir the mix as you add until it reaches the consistency of peanut butter—the new homogenized variety, not the old-fashioned type that's impossible to spread, and definitely not the crunchy type.

You can use a hefty stick or a margin trowel to stir with, but whatever you do, don't try the hand method. It's a mess. Thin set must be thick enough to stand up when spread with a notched trowel but not so thick that it's difficult to spread. You'll want the ridges to reach up and grip the bottoms of the tiles. Allow the mix to stand for 10 minutes, then remix. This ensures that dry ingredients are completely saturated with water.

The open time of thin set is considerable—two to four hours depending on surrounding temperatures—so don't get in a hurry. And besides, you've only made a small amount.

Begin spreading thin set in the grid square farthest from your access to the room. The size of the notched trowel depends on the undersurface of the tiles. If they are heavily corrugated, a $^3/_8$-inch trowel will usually do the job. If the tiles are relatively flat on their backs, a $^1/_4$-inch notched trowel will work. Saltillo and terra-cottas require a $^1/_2$-inch trowel at the least.

Scoop the mud out of the bucket with the end of the notched trowel and smear it on the floor. Don't be afraid to use too much; the excess will be picked up and returned to the bucket. Keep the trowel at about a 30-degree angle to the floor until the entire grid square is smeared with thin set. Go right to the lines, but don't cover them. Pay particular attention to the corners of the grid square, because tiles are weakest at their corners.

Now, turn the trowel up to about a 45-degree angle and go over the thin set to remove the excess, scraping the mud back into the bucket on its edge. You should have uniform ridges of mud over the entire grid square. These ridges ensure total contact with the bottoms of the tiles (FIG. 2-36).

2-36 Spreading thin set in a grid square.

Setting tile

Before you actually install the first piece of tile, you've got to remember which side of the line it's going to be set on. If you're in an entry or other room where the tiles have been centered, the centerline was made "off center" by half of a grout space. Therefore, if the line was made off-center" (to your left) the first tile will be placed with its edge "on" the line and to the left (see FIG. 2-29). If this tile were placed on the right side of the line, the field would be shifted by one grout space and the cuts along the walls would not be equal. An insignificant point you say? Since you've done everything perfectly up until now, why not continue?

Likewise, if you've got an "open" edge, the tiles are going to fit perfectly against that edge if they're full pieces. You might want to lay a grid of tiles "dry" to determine which ones are actually going to be set on the lines and which are to be set off the lines.

The first tile will be set at the intersection of two lines, and all other pieces in the square will be set off of it—the distance of a grout space. Set the pieces that fall on the lines first, then the ones that fall off the lines in the square. As you set each piece, move it back and forth a little to make sure it's firmly embedded in the thin set (FIG. 2-37).

2-37 First set the tiles that fall on the line.

If the square borders an edge, set all the full pieces first and then the cuts. Try to visually space grout joints so that the last tiles set in the square or those that are off the lines are one grout space away from the next line. You'll need that space when you set the adjacent square.

After all the tiles have been set in the square, concentrate on the spaces between them, and adjust the pieces so that all the spaces are equal. Scrape out any excess thin set from between the tiles. You can use the point of your buttering trowel or a margin trowel. Wipe thin set off the surfaces of the tiles with a sponge.

MAKING CUTS

Straight cuts are made with a cutting board. Don't leave cuts until later. Thin set begins to dry as soon as it's spread. This is called *overglazing*, and should it occur, the tiles won't bond properly to the thin set. Therefore, once the full pieces in a square have been set, it's time to make and install the cuts.

To accurately measure a cut, hold a piece of tile against the wall or baseboard with one edge parallel to it. Mark the tile with a pencil one grout space away from the last full piece it will be set next to (see FIG. 2-38). When cut and turned around, the cut edge should fit closely to the baseboard or the edge of the floor. The cuts don't have to be jammed up against the wall, but they should be fairly close—1/16 to 1/8 of an inch. When making the first cut, set the guide on the cutter so that repeat cuts can be made without having to mark them (FIG. 2-39).

2-38 Marking a cut.

As you're going along the wall, you'll probably have to adjust the size of the cuts slightly, because walls and baseboards are seldom perfectly straight. In cases where walls and baseboards are way out of line, you might have to turn the tile slightly in the cutter and cut on a bias to compensate for it. Mark the piece at both ends of the cut, and cut a straight line between the marks. Just don't get in a hurry. You only made a small amount of thin set, and its open time is considerable.

2-39 Making a cut.

Making L cuts

The process of cutting around corners is almost the same as making straight cuts. The piece is marked on one side and then turned around the corner where the other side of the L is marked. The difference is that the cutting is done on a saw instead of a cutting board. (See FIGS. 2-40 to 2-44.)

Let's take a moment to talk about saws and the proper way to use them. First, you've got water running in close proximity to an electric motor, which is a bad combination to begin with. Make sure your feet are dry when using the tool. Also, make sure that when you plug it in, the receptacle is grounded; otherwise, you might become the ground!

The blade itself won't cut you, but it is possible to get your finger caught between the blade and the table. This has never happened to me, but I imagine it would smart a little, and it could break a bone.

When cutting tile, glazed tiles especially, small particles can fly into your eyes. All saw manufacturers recommend the use of safety glasses. So, consider yourself warned.

The blade of a tile saw cuts by wearing away the material it comes in contact with; it really doesn't cut at all. The water running over the blade does two things. It keeps the blade from overheating, which would immediately ruin it, and it washes away the waste material created by the diamond chips, which actually do the "cutting."

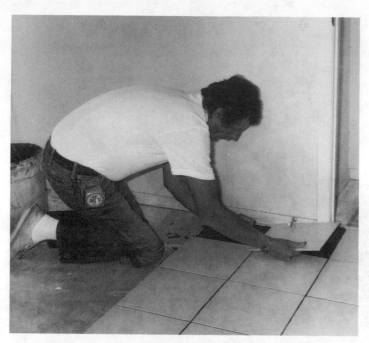

2-40   Marking an L cut.

2-41   Go around the corner and mark the other side of the cut.

2-42 The finished L cut.

2-43 Remove a tile and slide the L under the jamb.

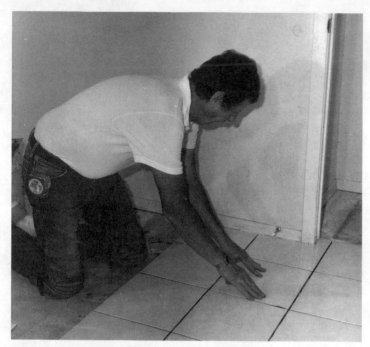

2-44 Reinstall the full tile.

The kerf, or width of the cut, is narrow, about $1/16$ of an inch. The piece being cut cannot be shifted or twisted on its way through the cut. In other words, you must cut in a straight line—the blade has minimal set. It's not like a woodworking blade at all.

When making L cuts, tilt the forward edge of the tile upward as it goes into the blade. This allows for getting into the corner of the L without leaving any residue. Keep the edge of the tile closest to you firmly implanted against the back guide of the table. If you try to lift it or turn it, the blade will bind in the kerf. If you're lucky, all that will occur is the blade will stall. If you're not, you could be seriously injured (FIG. 2-45).

I guess the key is: Don't get in a hurry. Although I consider using a tile saw much safer than using a woodworking saw, the accident potential is ever-present.

Now, let's get back to setting tile. The sequence in which you set the squares of your layout is not important but a matter of common sense. Don't wait until the last minute to do the areas behind doors. Do them while you still have enough room to maneuver. The same goes for closets. Closets can be done ahead of time before the main floor. This is another advantage of laying out the entire job before installing any tile. Just make sure you stay on the correct side of the lines. Follow the lines and everything comes together.

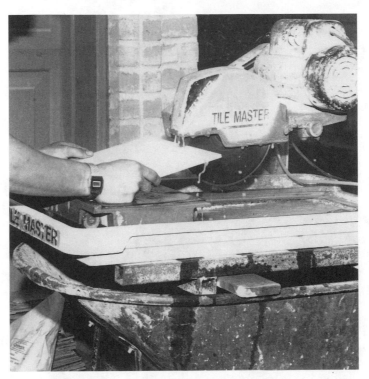

2-45 Using the tile saw.

Making cuts in doorways

Most entryways and many kitchens contain closets, which are usually tiled along with the main floor area. They are also at times adjacent to other floors that will not be tiled, and the transition from one floor covering to the other must be considered. The doorway is the most logical place for this transition. The tile runs halfway under the door when the door is closed.

The best way to handle doorways is to saw off the bottom of the door frame—jamb, casings, and all. The cut tiles are then pushed in under the jamb, and the actual cut is not seen. This can be done using a hand saw held flat to the floor atop a piece of scrap tile. The thickness of the saw blade will allow for the build-up of thin set under the cuts when they're installed. Because the cuts will be hidden, the only accurate cutting that must be done is along the baseboard or wall (FIG. 2- 46).

If the tile is to stop under the door, only that portion of the frame should be cut off and removed. When installing the cuts, a full tile is usually removed to allow room to slide the cut under the jamb. The full piece is then re-installed.

2-46 Cutting off the door casing.

The other method of getting around doorways is to cope, or notch, around the casing and jamb. This requires much trial and error. The piece is first rough cut and then fitted up against the casing visually. Then a series of smaller cuts are made with the saw and the biters until the cut fits snugly.

Patience is a key word in both methods, and satisfactory results are not always obtained on the first try. After ruining two or three pieces of tile, I usually stand around awhile and cool off. Muttering doesn't seem to help in this situation.

Making U cuts

By far the most difficult cut to make in floor work is the U cut. Tile setters go to great lengths during the layout stage to avoid having to make them, but sometimes, there's no other way to go.

The process is similar to that used in carpentry. A series of parallel cuts is made in the tile and the residue is knocked out of the way. The cut is then cleaned up with biters. U cuts generally occur when larger pieces of tile are used—12 × 12s and larger. If these cuts occur in a doorway, by all means, cut off the jamb and slide them under it. The accuracy needed to accomplish the job in any other way is, in many cases, not attainable by a professional—at least, not on the first try.

SETTING TILE RISERS

The vertical pieces of tile on a step can be buttered on with thin set. Use pieces of masking tape to hold them in place. Provide a grout joint between them and the horizontal pieces at the edge of the floor (See FIG. 2-22).

Use your buttering trowel to spread thin set on the backs of the riser tiles. Align their top edges with the edges of the tiles already set above them. Keep the riser tiles plumb by holding your level against them. Some of the pieces might require more thin set than others. Concrete risers are seldom exactly straight.

CLEANING UP

Now that all your tiles have been set, and you've stood around long enough to ensure the job looks good, it's time to wash the tools, clean up the work area, and prepare for another period of sitting around. The tiles should set overnight before they are grouted. Although tiles might become firmly set in a matter of hours, you'll want to make sure that the moisture in the joints has evaporated before you grout. Moisture has a definite effect on the final outcome of the grout. Also, you won't want to loosen any of the tiles from the mud bed by getting on them too soon.

Although there are quick-setting thin sets available, I don't recommend them. They're fine for a professional who has been doing the work for years but they set too fast for a novice. Besides, the mental pressure incurred might cut into your "Standing around" time, and you certainly don't want to rush the job. It takes the fun out of it, and it might cause you to get into the "It's good enough" attitude.

SETTING MEXICAN TILE

When setting tiles that are rustic in form and shape, the same principles of layout are employed except that the tiles must be set farther apart. Go through your stock of tiles and come up with a random sampling of pieces. Lay them out on the floor and allow for grout joints of about a $1/2$ inch. Measure a good portion of the tiles in your supply to ensure you're taking into account the largest pieces. It won't do to get halfway through the project and suddenly discover your tiles are getting bigger—the smaller ones will always fit.

Saltillo, terra-cotta, and other soft clay tiles must be cut on a wet saw; a tile cutter won't do the job. They are simply not stable enough to score and snap on the cutter. Therefore, arrange to have a saw available throughout the project.

Applying thin set

Mexican tile is not flat on the bottom and requires extra thin set. Thin set is applied with the largest notched trowel you can find. The backs of the pieces are buttered with additional thin set to ensure there are no voids beneath them when set. With Saltillo, the coverage is about 30 to 40 square feet per 50-pound sack of thin set.

Saltillo and many terra-cotta tiles are "thirsty," and this thirst must be slaked before they're installed or they'll draw the water from your thin set before it has a chance to cure. So, before you begin to set the tiles, stack them on the driveway and water them liberally with a hose until they are completely saturated. Let them stand a few minutes before installing them. The same process applies to grouting. Before you begin grouting, soak the tiles completely. The grout will harden the instant it hits the tiles. You can use grout release (available from tile suppliers) to prevent this from happening.

Grouting

Grout for Saltillo tiles is made the same way as mortar: one part portland cement to five parts masonry sand (5:1). Water is then added until the grout is soupy. If you want a finer texture on the surface of grouted joints, you can use silica sand, which is available at masonry supplies. Other than saturating the tiles, the grouting process is the same for any tile. Do a small area at a time, and wash it until it's clean.

Before attempting to seal or finish Mexican tile, it's necessary to wait at least three weeks to ensure that all water has evaporated. The tiles might look dry but moisture is still trapped within them. Don't be tempted to hurry the process. It might be necessary to wash the surface with a light acid solution to remove cement residue. See acid cleaning, chapter 7.

Chapter 7

Grouting floors

*G*routing floors is the process where cement is smeared over the entire surface of the floor and then cleaned up. Many people think grout is somehow applied to the joints only, but it is, in fact, spread over the surfaces of the tiles and forced into the joints with a rubber grout float. Prepared grouts are sold in 25 and 50-pound sacks. A range of colors is available and more are possible by blending two or more colors, although I don't recommend mixing colors. There are enough colors already available.

The grout we'll be using contains silica sand to give it extra strength because the joints are wider than $1/8$ of an inch. There are basically two types of sanded grout: one with latex added and one without it. Latex gives grout a degree of elasticity, making it stronger. Latex grouts are also more water-repellent than regular grouts.

If you're going to seal the installation with penetrating sealer, use a grout that does not contain latex. The sealer will be more readily absorbed into the joints. Whether you seal the floor depends on the type of tile. Dense tiles, such as single-fired glazed floor tiles, usually don't require sealer and some tiles are so dense they won't absorb it. Softer tiles such as Saltillo and terra-cottas, as well as some of the ceramics, should always be sealed, along with their grout joints. If the floor is not to be sealed, the latex type grout should be used.

Whether you seal the floor or not, keep in mind that the grout is going to get dirty no matter what you do to keep it clean. For this reason, I recommend using a color that is, as near as possible, the basic color of dirt. Browns, beiges, and grays work well. Aside from not readily showing dirt, they are neutral and won't interfere with the rest of your room decor. Of course, my advice isn't always taken, nor should it be, because grout color is a matter of preference. But I do usually succeed in convincing my customers not to use white grout on any floor. It'll be white for only a brief period of time and then it'll never be white again.

MIXING GROUT

Because this is probably your first time mixing grout, mix only a small amount. You can make more as you need it. It is, however, important to mix successive batches the same as the first. Water content has a definite effect on the final color and shade of the cured grout. Grout is basically mortar with color added and it'll set up at about the same rate as mortar.

Efflorescence

The water content of grout, as stated earlier, has a definite effect on the outcome of the job. Therefore, it is important to mix it the same way each time. Also, when washing, try to wash the entire floor consistently, even though you're washing small areas at a time.

Inconsistencies in grout shade occur most often with dense tiles—the tiles I've been advising you to use on your floor. The problem seems to be connected to the amount of water that remains in the joints after washing and how long it takes that water to evaporate. Grouting is never an exacting science, but try your best to control the water, both in mixing and in washing.

Efflorescence itself is a white looking deposit that accumulates on the surface of the joints when they are dry. Grout manufacturers employ chemists whose job is to determine what actually causes it, and to-date, nobody seems to know. But we do know it has to do with water. In many cases, it's possible to remove the deposit with a light acid solution after the grout has cured, but it's a chore. It's better to avoid the problem to begin with.

To mix the grout, pour about an inch of water into a clean bucket and add a little of the dry grout mixture. Alternate mixing and adding grout until you've got a creamy mixture. The grout should not contain excess water but it has to be smooth enough to ooze into all of the joints, including those between the cut tiles and the baseboards. If it's too runny, it won't set up fast enough in the joints, and if it's too stiff, it won't be workable with the float. After the grout has reached the desired consistency, allow it to stand for 10 minutes and then re-stir it. Now you are ready to spread.

SPREADING GROUT

The problem you'll encounter with spreading grout is getting the grout in joints to set so that you can begin washing it while not allowing the grout on the surfaces of the tiles to dry to the point that it can't be washed off. The harder or denser the tiles, the longer it takes for the grout to set enough to begin washing. There is a proper time to begin washing, and you'll have only one chance. If you start too soon, you'll wash down the joints, and if you wait too long, the tiles themselves will be extremely difficult to clean.

Start with a very small area, one you can clean up in a hurry if you have to. An area of about 4 to 6 square feet sounds good. If things get out of control, you can always wash out the grout completely and start over. In this sense, washing too soon is preferable to washing too late. After experimenting with a small area to get the feel of it, you can go on to bigger and better things.

Smear a test area with grout using a grout float. Keep the bottom of the float at a low angle to the floor. As you smear the grout, the angle of the float will force it down into the joints, bursting any air pockets that might be trapped under the grout (FIG. 2-47). When you're satisfied that all the joints have been filled, including those by the walls, turn the float to a higher angle and scrape as much grout as possible from the surface (FIG. 2-48).

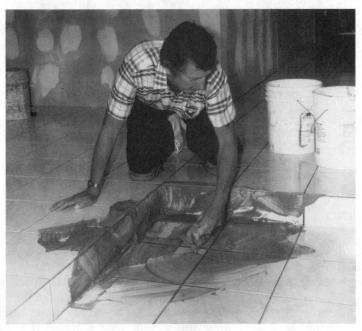

2-47 Smearing the grout.

Make sure you don't remove any of the grout from the joints. Keep the float working diagonally to the joints, not parallel to them. Now, clean your tools and wait for the grout to set. While you're waiting, get a sponge and a couple of buckets of water ready.

Aside from the density of the tiles, weather conditions determine the length of time it takes for the grout to set. If it's hot and dry, it won't be long. If it's cool and humid, it'll take longer. Test the joints from time to time by pushing your finger into one or two of them. When the grout begins to firm up, it's time to start washing. The grout won't be hard but it'll be stiffer, and most of the water in the joint will have evaporated. Under no circumstance should the floor be left unwashed for more than 30 minutes.

2-48 Rake off the excess.

WASHING

The first thing to do once grout is set is to get most of the grout residue off the surfaces of the tiles. Wring the sponge out so that it's not dripping and wash over the entire surface of your test area. Don't push down too hard into the joints. Rinse the sponge frequently and the work will go faster (FIG. 2-49). After you've removed most of the grout from the surface, start concentrating on the joints. Try to look only at the joints and ignore the tiles themselves. Each time the sponge passes across the joints, it removes a little of the grout. You'll notice that the joints begin to straighten and become smoother looking.

When washing, don't concentrate on any one joint, but keep the sponge moving over the entire area. This helps maintain continuity. As the level of the grout approaches the edge, or "shoulder," of the tile, it's time to stop. The idea is to keep the level of the grout as close to the surface as possible while still straightening the joints.

When the joints are straight and uniform, rinse the entire surface with clean water. Wring the sponge thoroughly and rinse it after each pass. One or two passes over the surface should do the trick (FIG. 2-50). Now, allow the surface to dry. Use the time to clean out your buckets and get clean water.

As the surface begins to dry, it'll "haze over," and the grout residue will become visible. Sometimes, when completely dry (20 to 30 minutes),

2-49 Begin washing.

2-50 Rinse the surface.

the haze can be wiped off with a dry cloth. If this is the case, that's all you have to do. Sprinkling a few drops of Old English lemon oil on a cloth will help pick up dust.

If the edges of the tiles begin to smear when you begin wiping, stop. Abandon this process. Instead, rinse the surface again with clean water, wringing the sponge thoroughly, and rinsing it after each pass. Allow the surface to dry, and rinse it again. At this point, you've done all you can do. There might be a slight residue, but if there is, it can be scrubbed off with soap and water after the grout has cured for a couple of days. When you're satisfied you've mastered the technique, go on to the next area, and repeat the process.

In an entryway or other small area, a professional would smear grout over the entire floor before beginning the washing process, but I don't recommend you do this. You could, however, work on more than one small area at a time. One area could be setting up while you're washing another, etc. But whatever you do, don't let it get ahead of you. A beautiful floor can be ruined by a sloppy grout job, and if it's allowed to cure, there's really no remedy for it. I'll say it again—take your time and keep your composure. You're on the final leg of the journey, and you're almost home.

FINISHING UP

Congratulations! You are now a tile setter, and more important, you're a mud man or woman, and it's something to be proud of. You've done the job the best way it can possibly be done, and it will last a lifetime. Just don't stand around wondering whether you should have used a different grout color. . . .

The grout will lighten in color in the next day or so and the residue on the surface, if any, can be scrubbed off with soap and water. Use Spic-n-Span or TSP. Do not use anything that contains an abrasive. If you can't get the film off in this manner, you can go back to the tile store and buy a small container of sulfamic acid crystals, but this should be a last resort. You must wait a couple of weeks before using the acid.

A word of caution

Some tiles, though not most, should not be cleaned with acid. It depends on what went into the glaze during manufacture. Check with your tile supplier as to the tiles you've chosen and whether acid might damage them. Wait at least two weeks before using acid on any installation because the grout must partially cure.

Acid cleaning

Acid attacks the calcium in cement, so it'll not only remove the film from the surfaces of the tiles but a thin layer of grout from the tops of the joints. Some tile setters use muriatic acid, and I hope they know what they're doing. A much safer bet is sulfamic acid because you can't over-concentrate it. When you add the sulfamic acid crystals to water, the water

will absorb only a certain number of them, and the rest will settle to the bottom of the bucket, remaining intact. But it's still acid and care must be taken when using it.

I know you've heard this before: Read the information on the container. Wear rubber gloves to prevent a severe case of dishpan hands, and keep the solution away from your eyes. Also, provide plenty of ventilation and try not to inhale the fumes.

Before you begin cleaning with acid, you'll need two buckets, one for the acid solution and one for clean water. You'll also need two sponges. Begin by saturating a small area of the grout joints with water. This prevents them from soaking up too much of the acid solution, which might weaken them. Again, don't try to do the entire floor area at once, but work a smaller area as you did when grouting.

Once the grout joints are saturated, dip the sponge into the acid solution and wring it out so that it does not drip. Begin washing the surface of the tile. The film will wash off almost immediately, and this is the time to thoroughly rinse the surface with clean water. Do a good job of rinsing before going on to the next area. You're not only picking up the acid and grout residue, you're diluting the acid that remains in the joints, which will dissipate as the water evaporates.

How do you dispose of the remaining acid in the bucket? You might consider cleaning up the mess you made in the driveway when mixing mortar or you can dump it, just be sure it's environmentally safe. Whatever you do, don't dump it in the flower bed or on the lawn. I guarantee you, this is not the type of acid that some plants thrive on.

MASONRY SEALERS

One of the questions asked frequently is, do I need to seal my floor? The answer is yes and no. If you've used hard, single-fired glazed tiles or porcelain tiles, the answer is no, because most single-fired tiles are so dense that sealers won't penetrate them. Sealers will just make a gummy mess on the surfaces of very dense tiles. Therefore, the challenge is sealing the grout without getting the sealer on the tile. You could use an artist's brush on the joints, being careful not to mess up the tiles; or spread sealer over the entire floor and clean it from the tiles; or you could simply use the grout that contains latex, and not worry about sealers.

As I said earlier, when latex is added to grout, it gives it a higher degree of elasticity, making it stronger. A side effect is that latex gives grout a degree of water-resistance, and hence, stain-resistance. The word is stain-resistant, not stain-free. The latex affords you a wipe up time when something's been spilled on the floor. If you wipe up the spill, you won't have any problems.

On the other hand, if you've used softer tiles—glazed or unglazed—sealing them is definitely in order. Check with your supplier and get a penetrating sealer. Applying sealer is much easier than painting a wall. Use a paint brush around the edges to keep it off the walls, and roll the rest of the floor with a roller. It's as easy as that.

Part 3

CERAMIC TILE WALLS

When we think of tiled walls, we naturally think of the bathroom, although tiled walls are used in many other areas of the home. How about a wainscot in the breakfast area or decorative tile on a wall in the sun room? A tiled door frame might be just the ticket to spruce up that drab entryway.

Numerous possibilities arise if the mind is allowed to wander, but because most ceramic tile walls are, in fact, in the bathroom, let's start there. One of the most obvious projects is a tub surround, and when you've mastered the techniques necessary to complete it, you'll be ready for any other project that comes to mind. So even if you're not planning to tile your tub area, read on, and later, I'll go into the specifics that are peculiar to other areas of the home.

I do not, however, discuss building and tiling complete ceramic tile shower stalls. There are tile setters who have been on the job for years who have not mastered the skills necessary to complete a project of this magnitude. It would take another book to impart the required information.

In the last 30 years or so, there's been a major increase in the cost of home building while the selling price of homes has not increased at the same rate. I'm referring to most of the country, certainly not those areas where housing costs have soared out of sight. But the fact is, the home builder, and I know you'll feel very sorry for him, is faced with a dilemma.

Consumers absolutely demand ceramic tile in the bathroom, built-in appliances in the kitchen, and in my area, you can't sell a house if it doesn't have a fireplace. And I live in the Sun Belt! At the same time, the builder has to watch his selling price or his competitors will shoot him out of the saddle.

Consequently, builders have come up with a workable solution. Give the home buyer ceramic tile, but don't install it over a proper substrate. Put in a fireplace, but make it "zero clearance," not a true masonry one. Many new and "improved" materials have been incorporated into the building process. Improved meaning cheaper. And the blame is shared equally by builders and consumers, but the buyer should be informed of what he's getting for his money, and that, my friend, is not the case, especially in the area of ceramic tile.

When you walk into the bathroom of almost every new home in the country, you're going to see ceramic tile around the tub and shower area, and it's going to look exactly like tile has looked for decades. But there's an excellent chance, if the home is not custom-built, that the tile has been installed over nothing but sheetrock, or plaster board. Imagine something that's wet all of the time simply glued to a piece of paper. Ceramic wall tile is not water-proof, and if it were, moisture would get behind it in the form of condensation. If the shower is used daily, it takes slightly more than two years for the tiles to loosen and begin to fall off the wall. Two years is the maximum period of warranty offered on a new home, and depending on who finances it, it might be only one year.

Should there be a law against the practice of installing tile over nothing but sheetrock in the bathroom? You bet. Is there a law? No. In fact, the installation of tile on sheetrock in bathrooms meets the building codes of almost every metropolitan area in the United States. Why? I don't know.

A ceramic tile shower or tub surround should last a lifetime. That's what you would expect of it and it will if it's done the old-fashioned way—over cement mortar—mud. And because you'll be providing the labor, it won't cost much more than a sheetrock job. It will, however, require time and physical effort, but when it's finished, you'll be able to call yourself a mud man, though you might be a woman, and there aren't that many of us left.

Chapter **8**

Wall preparation

*I*n the course of setting tile, sheetrock is sometimes used, but only as a backing material for the lath and mortar that actually becomes the structural wall behind the tile. If you're adding a new bathroom or if you're replacing sheetrock in a wet area, make sure it is the water-resistant type. In an area that's going to be covered with tile, such as a tub area, the joints do not have to be taped and finished. The metal lath that will be applied will provide plenty of continuity.

If you're working in an existing bathroom and don't know what type of sheetrock was used, you'll need to apply a moisture barrier to the walls in the areas that are going to be covered with tile. The best material to use is four mil sheet plastic, which can be tacked up on the wall. It is available in various size rolls at home centers and hardware stores.

In the tile setter's trade, a tub surround is called a *splash*, and that's the word I'll use to describe it from here on.

REMOVING EXISTING TILE

If your tile was installed over nothing but sheetrock, removing it won't be difficult. There are often two layers of rock behind the tile. One is part of the wall itself; the other was added in the area behind the tile. You can break a tile and remove it to determine whether there is sheetrock or cement mortar behind the tile. If it's sheetrock, all you have to do is remove it, tile and all. Just be careful not to destroy the layer of rock behind it. The original layer of rock will become the backing for the new installation. And don't "ding" the tub. It costs about $100 per ding to have it repaired. I'm speaking from experience.

Removing existing tile from a bath

The tile on a tub splash is always installed in a certain sequence: first the back wall and then the end walls. So in removing it, you should remove the end walls before you attempt to remove the back wall.

If the tile lies flat against the wall, it's probably just glued to the layer of rock that forms the bathroom wall. In this case, you've got two choices. You can cut around the edges of the tile and remove the tile and sheetrock together, and of course, install new sheetrock, or you can try to remove the tiles from the sheetrock—it depends on the type of adhesive that was used. In some cases, the tiles were attached with thin set and they'll be difficult to remove. Other times, mastic was used and tiles will come off fairly easily. The claws of a hammer will do the job and a margin trowel pushed behind the tile will aid in prying it off. Remember to protect the tub and make sure the drain is plugged before you begin.

NOTE: If you're going to be re-using the existing shower valve, take note of the size and shape of the openings after you remove the handles. You'll need to make your openings the same size when you're re-tiling the splash.

If mortar is behind your tile, you're in for some aggravation. Mortar is meant to stay in place (as I've mentioned) and getting tiles out is a real trick. You'll have to break the wall with a heavy hammer into manageable pieces because the entire installation weighs about 700 or 800 pounds, and obviously, you won't be able to remove it in entire wall sections. Six or eight square foot sections can normally be managed.

With a hammer and chisel, remove some of the trim pieces from the edge of the splash so that you won't destroy any walls that won't be hidden by the new tile. Try to pry loose a section at a time. You'll need tin snips to cut the metal lath or chicken wire that's embedded in the mortar. Wear gloves to avoid cuts and abrasions.

You might find this process too time-consuming and elect to remove the sheetrock also. Sometimes it takes less time to nail up a couple of pieces of rock than it does to save the old stuff and sheetrock is inexpensive.

MUD JOBS—THEN AND NOW

Before you actually start preparing the walls for the new installation, I think it appropriate to briefly describe a mud job and the processes necessary for its completion. Then we'll go through the project step by step. For as long as tile has been installed in bathrooms, its been installed over cement mortar—mud. So, I suppose, at least in our country, it has been around as long as inside plumbing. Mud must be reinforced to make the installation stronger and to keep it from cracking when the walls ''breathe'' or move due to settling. For years, metal mesh, chicken wire, or metal lath has been used for reinforcing.

In the days of plaster walls, lathers were responsible for installing the lath and plasterers provided a first coat of mortar, the ''scratch'' coat. The scratch coat was troweled on roughly and then its surface roughed up, or scratched, so that the next coat of mortar would adhere to it. Tile setters then floated the final coat of mortar, the ''brown'' coat, when they were about to install the tile.

In these older installations, the combined thickness of the various coats of mud might be 1¹/₂ inches thick. If you've got something like this to tear out, you're in for a shock. I compare it to trying to dismantle the proverbial brick outhouse.

In most cases, the tile, then and now, is set into wet mortar so that it can be beaten in with a beating block. It's a good way to ensure the tiles are even or flush with each other, producing a sleek, even, finished product. It is possible to let the mortar harden before installing the tile but extreme care must be taken to smooth the mortar before it sets. Once mud has hardened, it's difficult to correct a flaw.

With the advent of sheetrock walls, the scratch coat was eliminated and the lath or wire simply stapled or nailed to the sheetrock. It's still an excellent installation and will last indefinitely if properly done. This is the way I do tub splashes and I guarantee them for life.

CEMENT BACKER BOARD

As an alternative to lath and mortar, you could consider using cement backer board. Is it as good as lath and mortar? Absolutely not. Is there anything that compares to a real mud job? No.

Cement backer board is made from lightweight concrete reinforced with fiberglass netting. It is $1/2$ an inch thick, the approximate thickness of a mortar installation. The sheets measure 3×5 feet—5 feet being the length of a standard bath tub. You can purchase cement backer board at tile supplies, lumberyards, and home centers. The cost is about $1 per square foot or $15 per sheet. It takes the better part of four sheets to do a standard 5-foot tub splash.

Backer board is nailed over sheetrock with galvanized roofing nails. The boards can be cut by heavily scoring one side and breaking the sheet or by using a circular saw and masonry blade. The backer board is then nailed to the wall studs through the sheetrock using 2-inch galvanized roofing nails. Fiberglass joint tape is then used to increase continuity. Follow the manufacturer's directions.

You must figure the area to be tiled accurately and cut the material accordingly. The edges of the installation must be held back about $3/4$ of an inch to allow for the curved portion of the trim pieces that complete the tile installation. The tile process itself is identical to that for a mud job.

The advantage of the cement backer board is obvious—no wet mortar—but there are also disadvantages. To begin with, there are the joints. In a mud job, there are none. Metal lath is wrapped around the corners of the splash and every piece of lath is overlapped onto the next. The end result is monolithic. Then there is the question of straightness. Cement backer board is nailed up against a sheetrock wall that might not be straight and plumb. In a mortar installation, the walls are plumbed and straightened as the mortar is applied. Finally, cement board has not been around long enough to withstand the test of time, although I'm not saying it won't last. Cement mortar has existed since the days of the Roman Empire—well over 1,000 years—and much of that mortar still exists.

Should you use cement backer board on your project? If you don't feel you can handle the complexities of a mud job, and only then, yes. It's much better than gluing tile directly to sheetrock, and if it is done properly, it should hold up for a number of years.

There is nothing as good as a mud job, so give it a try. You can always remove the lath and nail up cement backer board if you decide you can't cope with floating the mud.

SYNTHETIC WALL MUD

Several manufacturers make synthetic mortars for use on walls in place of conventional mortar. The products are portland cement-based and contain various types of lightweight aggregate—no sand. Are they as good as regular, old-fashioned mortar? Take a guess. Besides not having withstood the test of time, they're expensive. A 50-pound sack costs about $12 to $15 and it takes four or five sacks to do a standard tub splash.

I don't want you to think I'm against every new product that comes on the scene, that is not the case. If the product does the job as well as the product it replaces and makes the work easier, I'm all for it. On the other hand, if the new product only makes the work go faster and it sacrifices durability, I'll spend hours, days, and years campaigning against it.

PREPARING THE SURFACE

The first thing to figure out in preparing the surface is how much of the wall is going to be tiled, and then establish those limits. A standard tub splash extends about 5 feet above the top of the tub. If you're going to be using standard 4¼-inch wall tile and 2-inch trim (A-4200), the height will be 5 feet 2 inches. Of course, you can go higher—to the ceiling if you like—it's up to you. Just be sure that the showerhead is completely surrounded by tile.

Using a level, draw a pencil line around the top of the area 1 inch below the actual top edge of the finished splash. This will be the line that the moisture barrier and lath will be cut to. You can lay a row of tiles out on the floor and measure them to determine the height of the splash. Don't forget the trim piece that will be installed at the top. If you're using standard 4¼-inch tiles, it takes 14 of them for a 5-foot splash.

The vertical edges of a splash usually extend a couple of inches beyond the front of the tub and the tile—usually bullnose (A-4200)—is run down to the floor (FIG. 3-1). You can come out farther if it suits you. Just be sure to lay out a row of tiles on the floor and determine what size cuts will abut the back wall. Preferably, you don't want the cuts to be less than half a tile.

Hold the level vertically and make a plumb line ½ inch back from the edge of the splash, from the floor to the horizontal line at the top. This is the line that the lath will be cut to. The reason for holding the lines inside the splash is so that there's no chance of getting the lath in the way of the portion of the bullnose that will curve around the edge of the mortar and return to the wall (see FIG. 3-2).

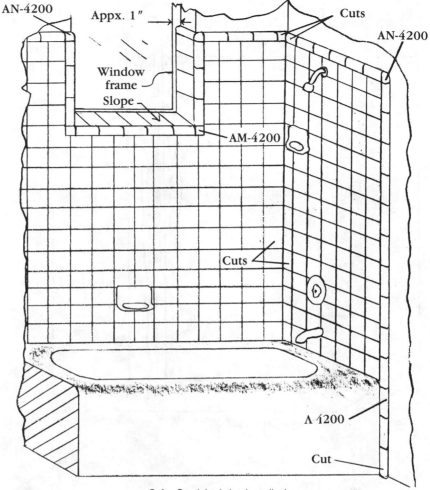

3-1 Straight joint installation.

MOISTURE BARRIER

If your sheetrock is not water-resistant, you'll need to protect it with sheet plastic. It doesn't have to be put up in one piece but the edges of the pieces must overlap by at least 2 inches. Go right to the lines you've established, and tack it in place with staples or roofing nails. Cover the entire area to be tiled.

METAL LATH

As discussed in Part 2, expanded metal lath is sold at masonry and tile supplies and comes in sheets of 26 inches by 8 feet. When installed, the sheets are overlapped 2 inches. It takes four sheets to do a 5-foot splash. If

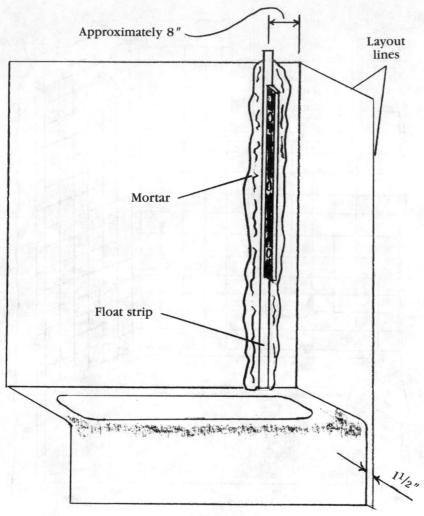

Approximately 8"

Layout lines

Mortar

Float strip

1 1/2"

3-2 Layout lines.

you can't find the lath, you can use galvanized chicken wire (poultry mesh) instead. Cut the pieces to extend from the top of the tub to the horizontal line or to the ceiling, if you're going that high. Begin applying it at the vertical lines at the front edges of the splash and work your way around towards the middle of the back wall, overlapping the joints 2 inches for continuity. Hanging the sheets vertically is easier than hanging them horizontally.

The lath doesn't have to be nailed into the studs, so you can use a staple gun to fasten it. The fasteners should be about 6 inches apart in both directions, horizontally and vertically. Position it fairly flat to the wall so that it won't get in your way when you're floating the mortar. Now, cut the narrow strips that go down the "legs" to the floor in front of the tub. Make sure they're overlapped onto the larger pieces of lath already installed.

If there is a window in the splash, treat it the same as the walls, remembering that the lath is always overlapped. If you don't have a staple gun, roofing nails work well. The window opening must be about 1 inch wider on all sides than the anticipated finished opening because the combined thickness of mortar and tile will be slightly less than 1 inch. Make sure you have this clearance before you install the lath inside the opening. If necessary, the sheetrock, if any, can be removed from the sill, window jambs, and header. If you get down to bare wood, protect it with a moisture barrier (FIG. 3-1).

Now that the "armature" has been installed, you're about to become a mud man, or woman. It might be a good idea to wait until the next day to continue the project because it's probably going to be an all-day job. Once you begin floating the mud, there's no stopping. It has to be done in one application to ensure continuity. This might be a good time to stand around and think about it.

Chapter 9

Floating walls

*T*he methods and materials for applying wet mortar to a vertical surface are much the same as for plastering a wall. The difference is in the tolerance. A plaster wall is usually painted and slight variances are not noticeable. Not so with ceramic tile walls. Grout lines exaggerate mistakes made when floating the walls. Is a tile setter a plasterer? Yes. Is a plasterer a tile setter? Not quite.

FLOAT STRIPS

It's not possible, even for a professional, to simply trowel mortar onto a wall and expect it to come out flat enough to install tile over it. The process entails applying more mud than needed and then raking the excess off with a straightedge. Something is needed to guide the straightedge near both ends of the wall while raking off the excess mud. Float strips, which are nothing more than pieces of wood lattice, 1/4-inch thick × 1 1/2-inches wide, are used for just such a purpose. The strips should be slightly longer than the height of the wall being floated or, if you're going to the ceiling, about an inch shorter so that they'll fit in easily. The strips are tapped into wet mortar with a level held against them to get them plumb, or vertical. You'll need two.

MORTAR BOARD

Before you can begin floating mud, you've got to figure out how to hold the mortar board up at a convenient height. I usually stack boxes of tile to a height of about 30 to 36 inches and then balance the board on top of them. This works fine if the mud is always dumped right in the middle of the board. If not, there are problems. You can make a stand for your board out of scrap lumber. It doesn't have to look great; it just has to be strong enough to do the job. Anyway, position your mortar board in the middle of the floor, just outside the tub so that you can easily reach it without having to climb out of the tub every time you need a load of mud.

All of the wooden tools—float strips, straightedges, and the mud board—must be wet before use so that they won't draw moisture out of the mud. Bring in a half a bucket of water with a sponge in it to wet them. You'll also need the water nearby to wash things from time to time as well. You should have two straightedges, one about 4$^{1/2}$ feet long for the back wall and one about 3 feet for the end walls.

MIXING THE MUD

Before you begin mixing mud, make sure all the "standing around" is out of your system because there won't be any time for it until you've finished. The mud goes up in one continuous operation. A tile setter would immediately begin installing the tile as soon as he was finished with the mud work, but it doesn't have to be done that way. It is much easier for a novice if the mud is allowed to harden overnight.

The mortar you'll be using is called *wall mud* and is also referred to as *fat mud* because it contains lime in addition to masonry sand and portland cement. Again, you have two choices. You can use portland cement, lime, and sand or you can purchase masonry cement, which already contains lime. I've been using masonry cement for the past several years, and it's much easier than carrying around all the other products. So, I suggest using masonry cement, but I'll give you the ratio for the portland method just in case you want to do it that way. It is: one part portland cement and one part construction lime to five parts masonry sand. The amount of water needed depends on the moisture content of the sand when you begin. It's a type of guessing game that I'll explain when the time comes. All of the ingredients can be purchased at masonry supplies.

Masonry cement is sold in 70-pound sacks, and the recipe we'll use is: eight heaping shovels of sand to half a sack of cement. This is a small batch suitable for a wheelbarrow and probably as much as a beginner should mix at one time. A standard 5-foot-high splash can normally be completed with two of these batches, or one sack of masonry cement. If you're going higher than 5 feet, you'll need two sacks.

Measure the sand into the wheelbarrow or mixing box—eight good shovels of sand. Then add half a sack of masonry mix. It's important to dry mix the sand and cement before adding the water. This ensures that the sand particles are completely coated with cement. It's best to use a hoe for this. If you don't have a masonry hoe, a garden hoe will work; it'll just take a little longer. Chop down at the mix, working from one end to the other. Continue chopping it back and forth until the particles are coated with cement (FIG. 3-3).

When the sand is well coated with cement, it's time to add the water. Start with about 2 gallons of water and go from there. The capacity of the plastic buckets I've talked about is 5 gallons. So, if you fill one slightly less than half way, you'll be close to the 2-gallon mark. It will probably be nec-

3-3 Dry mixing the mud.

essary to add more but this will get you started. If your sand is very wet (it might have been rained on the night before), add only 1 gallon of water to begin with (FIG. 3-4).

Now, repeat the chopping motion with the hoe. Work the mix back and forth, reaching all the way to the bottom. Your mix should be buttery but not watery. The mortar must be smooth enough to work with a trowel but not runny. It should stand up on the mud board without slumping much, so don't overdo it with the water. It's much easier to add a little more water than it is to fix the mix by adding more sand and cement. Add water a quart or two at a time.

If you're familiar with the mortar used by brick masons, make yours slightly stiffer because you won't have the bricks to soak up the excess water. When the mud's consistency is correct, fill two buckets about half full and carry them into the bathroom. Any mud left outside should be covered with something, such as plastic, to help prevent moisture loss due to evaporation. The mud will be usable for an hour to an hour and a half, but after that, it should be discarded. That's why it's a good idea to keep the batches small.

After making sure the mud board is wet, dump one of the buckets of mud on it. Stretch a couple of times to get all the kinks out of your body—the fun is about to begin.

3-4 Measure the water.

HAWK AND FLAT TROWEL

It is almost impossible to learn from a book the proper use of a hawk and trowel. It takes years of doing it regularly to get good at it, and you're going to have to learn cold turkey. The edge of the hawk is laid on the surface of the mud board beside the pile of mud. The mud is then pulled up onto it with the flat trowel. Don't completely load the hawk, just take it slow until you get the feel of it (FIG. 3-5). Holding the hawk level, turn around and face the back wall. You're about to find out that getting the mud onto the hawk is much easier than getting it off and onto the wall. Generally, the hawk is tipped toward you at the same time the trowel scoops off a portion of the mud. The trowel now has to be held level to prevent the mud from sliding off before it reaches the wall. Hold the trowel loosely, with the backbone of it resting against the backs of the upper part of your fingers.

Oops . . . the mud fell in the tub? Scoop it out of the tub with your hands and get it back on the board—and be more careful (FIG. 3-6). Easy for me to say, isn't it? What you're trying to do is to form a vertical path of mud from the top of the tub to the top of the splash, about eight inches out from either corner. This is where the float strip will be embedded. It doesn't matter if you start at the bottom or the top of the wall. Do what seems easiest for you (FIG. 3-7).

3-5 Load the hawk.

3-6 A ''forehand'' stroke.

3-7 Inserting the float strip.

Trowel the mud on about ¹/₂ inch thick. It might be easier if you load only one trowel-full onto the hawk at a time. Then, after you've gotten it onto the trowel, you won't have to worry about any falling off the hawk while you're troweling the mud onto the wall. Or, you can shove the edge of the hawk against the wall and push the mud up and away from it with the trowel. That way you can catch most of what falls. Don't scoop mud out of the tub with a trowel when it falls; it could leave permanent marks on the tub.

I know all of this doesn't sound very professional but I'm telling you all the things I did before I became proficient with the hawk and trowel. And they worked! I wasn't the fastest tile setter in the world (and I'm not now), but I got the job done and done right, and that's all you have to do. I won't tell you how long it took me to get really good at it . . . I don't want to discourage you. Just get the mud on the wall somehow, and the rest is easy. A professional can float a splash in an hour or less. If it takes you four hours, you're still doing fine. Just don't lose your composure.

When you get a little pathway of mud floated from the top of the tub to the top of the splash, you're ready to tap in the float strip. Make sure the strip is damp and then push it gently into the mortar. Try to get it vertical. Now, place the edge of the level against it and look at the plumb vial. With the butt of the handle of your buttering trowel or margin trowel, tap against the edge of the level, keeping an eye on the vial. You have to get the strip plumb and as close to the lath as possible (FIG. 3-8). Many tile setters use a small rubber mallet to tap the level with. I've never had one, but it'll work better than a trowel handle. You might have to tap quite hard to get the strip in where you want it. Ideally, you should end up with the surface of the strip a half inch from the sheetrock. A 1/2-inch mud bed is perfect but slightly more won't hurt.

3-8 Plumb the strip with the level.

If your wall is way out of plumb, you might not be able to plumb it with mortar. If you try to apply too much mud, the weight of it will pull it from the wall, and this is disheartening. About 3/4 of an inch, or slightly more, is the maximum amount of mud that can be applied at one time. Because the back wall of the splash is visually less critical than the end walls, it won't be noticed if it's a bit out of plumb, but that's only if it's impossible to plumb it.

Move the level along the float strip and repeat the tapping until the strip is straight and plumb or as close as you can get it if the wall is ''out.'' It's extremely important to get the strip straight, i.e., no humps or dips, even though it might not be exactly plumb. No one will notice a back wall that is a 1/4 to 1/2 inch out of plumb but everyone will see a 1/2 inch bow in the wall. So don't build any ski chutes; keep your walls straight at all cost.

That wasn't so hard, was it? All you have to do is repeat the process in the other corner. Set the float strip about 8 inches from the corner and plumb it with the level.

When you're satisfied that the float strips are properly set, you're half-way home. A tile setter would begin troweling mud at the top of the wall and work his way down. That way, he's not dropping mud on the portion he's already floated. But it might be easier for you to start at the bottom. In either case, you should fill the spaces between the strips and the corners before you fill in between the strips. Then you won't have to concentrate on the corners when you're floating the middle section of the wall.

Whether you start from the top or the bottom (or both), fill in the area between one strip and the corner. Be careful not to push on the float strip too hard with the trowel (FIG. 3-9). The mud must protrude slightly in front of the float strip. Now, with the straightedge held gently against both strips, scrape off the excess mortar. Don't push too hard against the strips, and work with an upward motion (see FIG. 3-10). Don't try to remove too much mud with each pass. Too much of a build- up on the straightedge might pull against the mud that you want to leave on the wall and cause it to fall into the tub—again. Use short strokes and dump the mud back onto the mud board. You can scrape the mud off the straight-edge with your margin trowel.

3-9 Float the area between the strip and the corner.

3-10 The straightedge must rest against both strips.

If you see voids in the surface of the mortar after you've used the straightedge, they must be filled in and scraped off again. These voids are known as "holidays," implying that the tile setter was on vacation when that portion of the wall was floated. It's better to have holidays than to have too much mud on the wall, however. If there's too much mud on the wall when you begin scraping it, you stand a good chance of pulling all the mud right off the wall, and we've been through that. It's a sad feeling, especially if it's taken a good deal of time to get the mud on the wall in the first place. Of course, it affords a great opportunity for more practice with the hawk and trowel.

Now, repeat the process in the opposite corner. After the end spaces have been floated, you can fill in the middle section of the wall and straightedge it. Remember not to put too much pressure on the float strips. You don't want to put a bow in the wall (FIG. 3-11).

If there is a window in the wall you're floating, pretend it's not there and float right past it to the top of the wall, then deal with the window. In fact, it might be even better to float the two end walls before you complete the window opening. This will allow time for the mud on the wall to partially set and you won't be as apt to damage it while floating the inside of the window opening.

Floating an end wall is the same as floating the back wall—almost. You should use some sort of "stop" at the outside edge to keep the mud

3-11 Float the area between the two strips.

from going beyond the edge of the splash. This can be a piece of wood quarter-round or anything that is 1/2 an inch thick. It can be nailed vertically to the sheetrock with three or four small nails outside the line at the edge. The nail holes will later be covered by bullnose, which will extend past them (FIG. 3-12). In addition to acting as a stop, this piece of wood can also be used as a "ground," meaning the straightedge can be held against it if the ground is plumb. This alleviates the need for one of the float strips. The straightedge will ride against the stop and a float strip located near the corner.

You can plumb the stop by placing shims behind it or even by pushing small amounts of mortar behind it. Hold the level against it to get it plumb (FIG. 3-13). Getting the end walls plumb is probably more important than plumbing the back wall. Aside from the visual effect, there are other considerations such as a tub enclosure (glass doors), which would be mounted directly onto the tiled surface. A variation of a 1/4 inch can usually be concealed, but not more. A bow in one of the end walls will visually jump out at you, whereas if the bow is in the back wall, it would be less noticeable. Regardless what shape the bathroom walls are in, the splash itself is the project. Make it as correct and as visually pleasing as possible. If your walls are so way out of plumb that you can't get the mortar plumb (within 1/4 of an inch), you must consider using a shower curtain instead of an enclosure. But keep the wall straight.

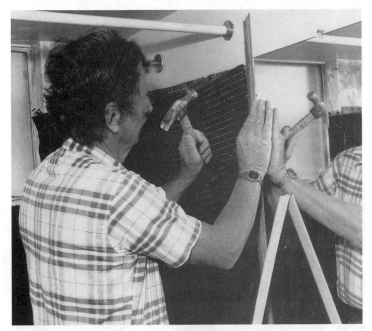

3-12 Installing the stop.

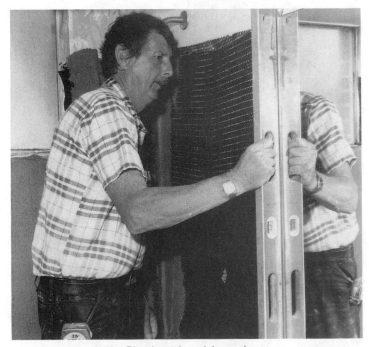

3-13 Plumb and straighten the stop.

3-14 Plumbing the float strip.

3-15 Floating the corner area.

Pry one of the float strips out of the back wall, scrape it off with your margin trowel, and re-set it in the end wall (FIG. 3-14). When your stop and your float strip are set, float the space between the strip and the corner first. Try not to dig into the mud on the back wall. Then float the rest of the wall (FIG. 3-15).

PLUMBING FIXTURES

Getting around valves and shower arms is a matter of turning the straight-edge back and forth out of the level position and taking short strokes to remove the excess mud from around the obstructions. The little bit of mud that remains around the valve or pipe can be left there for the time being. It'll be removed later when the mud has partially set (FIG. 3-16).

Take care to protect plumbing valve parts when mud is floated on the wall. A new valve comes with a plastic protector that also acts as a template for the opening left in the mortar. Make sure the protector is in place before floating the wall. If you will be using the existing valve, tape it with masking tape to keep the mud away. Also, you need to provide enough room around the valve or stems to facilitate changing parts after the tile has been installed. Stems can be wrapped with several layers of cardboard held in place with masking tape. Make the openings the same as the originals and you shouldn't have any problems.

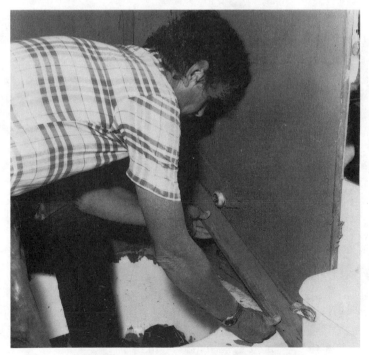

3-16 Getting around the tub-shower valve.

3-17 We're really moving now.

3-18 A little too much mud on the wall.

3-19 Troweling the "leg."

3-20 Careful not to scratch the tub.

BLOCKING THE WALLS

Once mud has been applied to all three walls and scraped even, the bulk of the mud work is done, but it's still necessary to do a little fine-tuning before the tile is installed (FIGS. 3-17 through 3-20.) First, float strips must be removed from the wall. Carefully remove the strips, fill the depressions, and scrape the mud smooth again (FIG. 3-21). Now, with the beating block held flat against the wall, rub the entire area to remove small humps and to further smooth the walls. Begin with the first wall you floated, which would be the back wall. You should wait a while before blocking the last wall you worked on. Give the mud a chance to partially set so there's no danger of pulling it from the wall (FIGS. 3-22 and 3-23).

3-21 Fill the depressions left by the float strips.

Hold the block between your fingertips and your thumb and begin working with a circular motion, moving the block around as you go. Avoid pushing so hard that the edge of the block digs into the mud. Don't spend too much time in any one spot or water will begin to float to the surface. A couple of passes should do the trick. Excess mortar can be cut off with the edge of the block. Don't try to force a lump of mud into the wall, cut it off instead. All you need do is remove the rough spots. You can

3-22 Block the walls right into the corners.

3-23 One or two passes does it.

work right into the corners and square them up. Also, now is the time to block around the plumbing fixtures to remove the excess mortar that was left there. Another area to concentrate on is just above the tub. Make sure the wall is straight, right down to the tub itself. You can check the wall with a straightedge held vertically. Don't forget the "legs" that run down to the floor in front of the tub.

FLOATING A WINDOW

In the tile setting trade, the inside surfaces of a window or door are referred to as *jambs*. There is the header, which is the upper surface. Then there are the side jambs and the sill. For reasons that will become obvious, the header or head jamb is by far the most difficult to deal with. A head jamb cannot be floated in one day because the mortar, in the required thickness (1/2 inch), is too heavy to stay up there. Therefore, the header must be scratched, meaning a thin coat of mud is applied and then roughed up so that a subsequent or finish coat can be applied, usually the next day. Therefore, if the tile is to go up past the window, the head jamb must be dealt with first.

Apply a thin coat of mortar on the head jamb, scratch it slightly with the edge of a notched trowel, and leave it alone. The following day, dampen the scratch coat with a sponge and float on the final coat of mortar.

As an alternative to floating the head jamb, you might consider using a piece of cement backer board. Cut it to fit and nail it securely to the header. Remember the curved trim must fit around the outside edge of it, so hold that edge back 3/4 of an inch from the surface of the mortar on the wall. Take pains to install the piece level—you might have to do a little shimming.

The two side jambs are floated next. Have your helper do this with you. Position a straightedge flat against the wall and plumb it with a level. The edge should protrude into the window opening about 1/2 inch. You must provide for the thickness of the tile after the mud is floated. Don't end up with the finished jamb protruding into a pane of glass (see FIG. 3-24).

When the straightedge is positioned and plumb, have your helper hold it while you apply the mud to the jamb (FIG. 3-25). Or, because your helper hasn't had any practice yet, maybe you should hold the straightedge and let him or her float the jamb. Just fill the area between the straightedge and the window frame. Now, if you're very careful, you can rake the mud off with the edge of the flat trowel. It doesn't have to be perfect, just close (FIG. 3-26). Repeat the process on the opposite jamb. Provide the same "reveal" on the window frame as you did on the other side jamb. In other words, center the window in the opening. Like the walls, the jambs can be smoothed after the mud has begun to set, just don't forget about them.

3-24 Plumb the straightedge with the level.

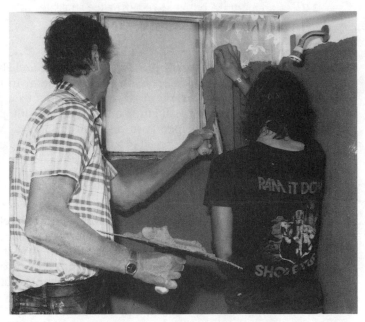

3-25 Have the helper hold the straightedge while you're applying the mud to the side jambs.

3-26 Carefully rake off the excess using the straightedge as a guide.

FLOATING WINDOWSILLS

Sills and other horizontal surfaces in a shower area are always floated slightly out of level so that water won't stand on them. In the case of a windowsill, because it is narrow, $1/8$ of an inch is adequate and $1/4$ of an inch is not too much. Float the sill the same way as the side jambs using a straightedge held by your helper. Position it with the level. When you're removing the excess mud, tilt the sill in towards the tub. Again, it doesn't have to be perfect; it can be touched up later. Just make sure there is more mud near the window, and that the sill tilts in towards the tub between $1/8$ and $1/4$ of an inch (FIG. 3-27).

For the most part, your mud work has been completed, and I can almost hear that big sigh of relief, but the job isn't completely done until everything's been washed up. Anything that comes in contact with cement must be washed off with water, including the tub itself. Remove the mud from the tub with your hands or a sponge. The inside surfaces of the window opening, if there is one, must be blocked off after about an hour.

As I mentioned earlier, it is better to wait until the next day to set the tile. The mortar must be completely smoothed off and blocked before you quit, however. Straighten out your window area if you have one, and make sure all the walls are straight. Check them with a straightedge once

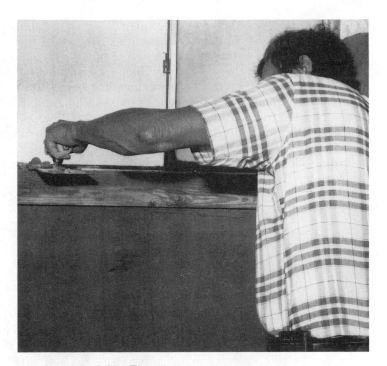

3-27 The sill tilts in toward the tub.

3-28 Trim the excess from the top of the splash.

more to be sure. The top edge of the splash must also be straightened (FIG. 3-28). If you're using standard $4^1/4$ tile with a 2-inch trim, the height of the mortar will be 5 feet $1^1/2$ inches above the tub. A few standard wall tile manufacturers make theirs $4^3/8$ of an inch instead of $4^1/4$. To be certain, lay a row of tiles out on the floor and measure them.

If you're using some other type of tile, you'll have to figure the total height plus the trim and then adjust the mud accordingly. The mud must stop about $1/2$ inch short of the desired finished splash so that it won't get in the way of the rounded portion of the trim. Figure the correct height and using a level as a guide, cut the excess mud off with a margin trowel. In short, anything that needs to be done is much easier done before the mud sets. You might want to stand around and admire your handiwork briefly, but don't overdo it, it's bad form.

Chapter **10**

Setting wall tiles

*B*efore you install the first piece of tile, you need to first consider the layout. If you're using standard wall tile, are the joints going to be straight or will the tiles be stacked like bricks with broken vertical joints? Should the back wall be centered? How are sheets of tiles installed? What about the window? Because standard wall tile is the most common, let's start there.

STRAIGHT JOINTS

If you were to start in one corner of a standard 5-foot tub and run a row of $4^1/4$ tile to the other corner, you would have to cut the last piece. This cut is usually about half a tile or slightly larger. If the tiles are to be set one on top of another with the vertical joints straight, the field of tile should be centered so that you will have equal cuts in both corners.

NOTE: If you were unable to plumb one or both of the end walls, the broken joint method discussed in the next section should be considered instead of the straight joint method. Because the vertical joints are not in line, the discrepancies in the end walls are less noticeable.

If you're using standard $4^1/4$, it takes 14 pieces to reach from one corner to the other, or seven pieces on either side of a centerline. The cuts in the corners will be larger than half a tile. If there is a window in the back wall, and the window is centered in the wall, or almost centered, it might be a better idea to equalize the cuts that will go up both sides of the window. The cuts in the corners of the splash will still be of almost equal size. If the window is off center, the size of the cuts along its sides aren't as important.

Measure to the middle of the back wall, and with the level held plumb, scratch a line to the top of the splash or to the windowsill with the edge of a trowel. It's easy to figure the size of the cuts this way, either at the window or in the corners of the splash. You can measure to each side

117

3-29   Position the centerline.

3-30   Holding the level plumb, scratch the centerline.

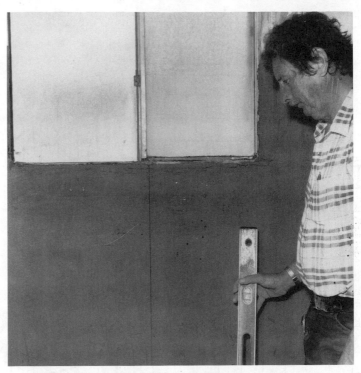

3-31 Line centered on the window opening.

of the window opening to see if its centered. If it's just a little off center, move the centerline to the center of the opening to equalize the cuts on its sides (FIGS. 3-29 to 3-31).

BROKEN JOINTS

There is an easier method of setting tiles other than straight vertical joints. It involves stacking the tiles like bricks with the vertical joints staggered on alternating courses, or rows (see FIG. 3-32). Broken joints are commonly used in new homes unless someone specifies otherwise.

Horizontal joints must be straight and level, but because vertical joints are not continuous, slight variations in alignment are not noticeable. And the field is almost always automatically centered when doing a standard 5-foot tub splash. Centering the field of tile is optional with this method. You could just start in one corner and go to the other. You'll have two different sizes of cuts from one course to the next. The beginning cuts (on alternating courses) will be halves.

LEVELING

Since I've already discussed centering the field of tile, you can get right into stacking the tiles themselves. Lay your level on the rim of the tub to deter-

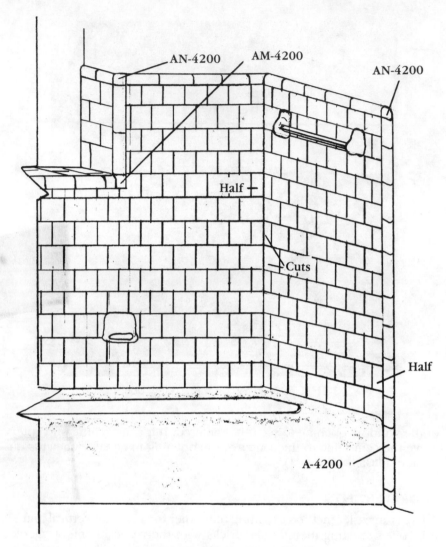

AN-4200   AM-4200   AN-4200

Half

Cuts

Half

A-4200

3-32 Broken joint installation.

mine whether it's truly level. If it is, you're very lucky, because it doesn't seem to happen that often (FIG. 3-33). If the back of the tub is within $1/8$ of an inch of being level, you can begin to set the tile. The first course of tile can be shimmed to get the row level. If the tub is more than $1/8$ inch out of level, tiles must be cut so that their top edges are level when set. This is important because in order to end up with straight joints from top to bottom, the tiles must be set level and plumb. There's no leeway.

At the low end of the tub, place a tile against the wall and rest it on the rim of the tub. Scratch a mark at the top of the piece with your margin trowel. Now, using the level with its top edge held on the mark, scratch a level line in the mortar. With the level, extend the line to the other end of

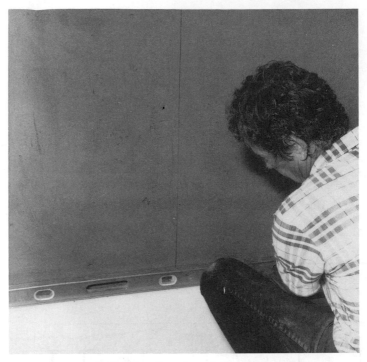

3-33 Checking the tub for "level."

the tub (see FIG. 3-34). Now, with your biters, trim off the bottoms of the first course of tile so that each piece just reaches the line when placed on the rim of the tub. And keep the pieces in proper sequence. This process is necessary for both the straight and broken joint methods when the tub is not level. Now it's time to mix the thin set.

MIXING THIN SET

You should be using the white thin set that is formulated especially for walls. Put a couple inches of water in the bottom of a bucket and add a little thin set. The consistency you're looking for resembles peanut butter—the new homogenized type. It can't be stiff or you won't be able to trowel it on the mortar. Add a little at a time and stir it. It's better to have it a little on the creamy side than to have it too thick. You can always stiffen it up later. Allow the mix to stand for 10 minutes and then re-stir. The open time of thin set is about two hours or so, and you've only mixed a small amount, so don't get in a hurry—keep your composure.

SETTING THE BACK WALL

Since your splash has set overnight, you might want to wet the mortar a little so that it doesn't dehydrate the thin set before you get the tiles

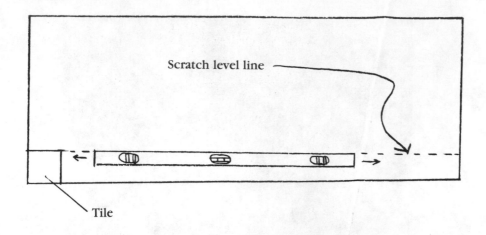

Scratch level line

Tile

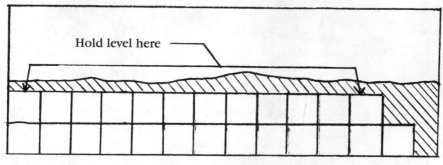

Hold level here

3-34 Leveling the field.

where you want them. Just splash a little water on the back wall with a sponge. Don't soak it.

Begin by setting three rows (courses) of tile along the top of the tub on the back wall. If you've already drawn your centerline, you're ready to go. If not, do it now. With a $1/8$-inch notched trowel, spread thin set on the wall from the top of the tub to a height of about 13 or 14 inches. Do not cover the centerline. Clean off any that drops on the rim of the tub. You don't want it under the bottom row of tiles. If you're using the straight joint method, begin setting tiles in both directions on either side of the line until you get to the cuts. If your tub is out of level, these will be the tiles that you've trimmed off. Don't worry about the end cuts at this time.

Stack another two courses of tile on top of the first course (FIGS. 3-35 to 3-37). Tap them in with the beating block held flat against the tiles, hitting the block with the butt of your trowel handle. You won't be able to tap them in too far so don't hit them hard (FIG. 3-38). Now you're ready to level them.

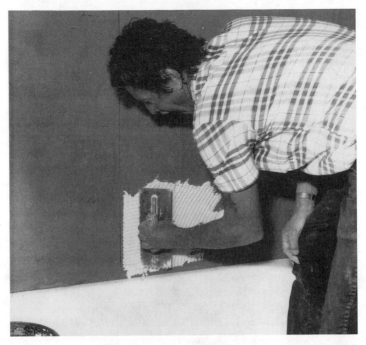

3-35 Spreading the thin set.

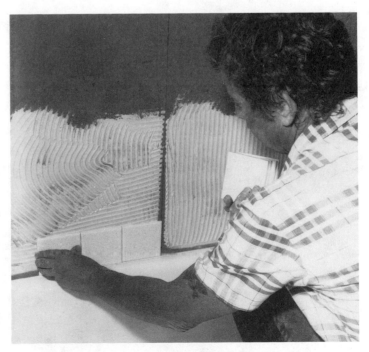

3-36 Begin setting the tile on either side of the center line.

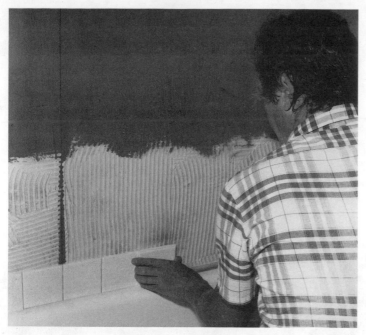

3-37 Are we having fun yet?

3-38 Using the beating block.

Have your helper hold the level on top of the tiles you've set so that you can work with both hands. With your buttering trowel (or margin trowel), pry between the top of the tub and the bottom tiles until the top course is straight and level. You can use pieces of cardboard as shims to hold them up. Plastic wedges are sold at tile supplies for this use and they work better than cardboard. However you do it, it's absolutely essential that the tiles be perfectly level (FIG. 3-39). Even though you've wet the wall, the tiles will draw moisture out of the thin set, so don't stand around at this time. Get them level and then put the cuts on the ends, making sure all joints are aligned (FIG. 3-40).

The cuts don't have to fit tightly against the end walls because the tiles on those walls will cover them. If you're using broken joints, the second course will be offset by half a tile. Now you can take a break, if you like.

3-39 Shimming the field to level it.

Overglazing

When thin set has been smeared on the wall, it immediately begins to dry on its surface. This is called *overglazing*. Depending on the room temperature, you'll have only a few minutes to set the tiles after smearing the mud. If tiles are set into thin set that has glazed over, they won't properly

3-40 Setting the end cuts.

bond. Check for this condition from time to time by lightly prying on a piece of tile. Don't pry too hard, however. If it's not bonded, it'll come off the wall easily. Remove all the tiles not bonded and scrape the old thin set from the wall. You can then either butter the tiles back on or spread new thin set..This is why it's a good idea to only spread enough thin set to accommodate three or four courses of tile at a time. And always stack the field before you worry about the cuts.

Tiles, like everything in life, are not perfectly made. There are minor variations in size, and you'll usually find glaze on some of the spacer lugs. What this means is that you'll have to adjust the tiles. Play with them as they're being set to keep them straight and level. You might have to move them sideways to keep the vertical joints straight and shim individual tiles from time to time to keep the horizontal joints level. This is done visually and it's where experience comes into play. Because you have little or no experience, you should stack only three or four courses at a time and then stop to straighten them out.

I've already stated that it's important to keep the courses level. It is equally important to keep the vertical rows plumb if you're setting straight vertical joints. The tiles are square and they won't give—even a little. If they are not set perfectly level and plumb, it's impossible to keep the joints straight.

Smear thin set far enough up the wall to set three or four courses of tile. Smear across the wall from one corner to the other. If you're right-handed, stack a vertical row of tile on top of the last full tile on the left-hand side of the wall, three or four tiles high. Now, with the level held vertically against the edges of the tiles, move them until they are plumb. This is your lead row of tiles and the remaining tiles will be set off them (FIG. 3-41). The field tiles are stacked later from left to right. If you are left-handed, it's easier to set the lead row on the right-hand side of the wall from right to left (FIG. 3-42). If you are using the broken joint method, you won't need the lead row because your vertical joints will be staggered.

3-41 Plumbing the lead row.

When three or four courses have been set, put in the cuts on the ends and tap the tiles in with the beating block. Don't beat the tiles that were set below them. The thin set will have partially set by now and the tiles might break loose.

You can adjust the tiles by moving them sideways or shimming between the tiles, jacking them up, in order to get the joints level and straight (FIG. 3-43). Rest the level on the top course and shim tiles up to its bottom edge. After about half an hour, the shims can be removed. The process is then repeated until you reach the top of the splash or the windowsill, if there is one.

3-42 Some of us are left-handed. Start at the other end if you're not one of us.

3-43 Shim the tiles level after each "lift."

Broken joints

As I stated earlier, eliminating straight vertical joints makes the work go much faster because you don't have to worry about keeping the vertical rows plumb. Horizontal courses must still be kept straight, however. After every three or four courses, rest the level on top of the field. Shim the tiles up to the bottom of the level. Remember, no ski chutes.

Begin setting the first course of tiles in a convenient corner, depending on whether you're right or left-handed. Start with a full tile; the cut will be on the other end. When you get to the other side, put in the cut. It'll be about a half of a tile. For the second course, begin with a half piece, with the cut edge facing the corner. Now, set the second row to the other corner. You should end up with a full tile in the opposite corner—or most of a tile—although you might have to bite it off a little. If the last tile doesn't quite reach to the corner, you can spread the tiles slightly, but spread them evenly. If this doesn't work, the field will have to be centered. This situation is rare in a 5-foot bath tub, however (FIG. 3-32). Continue setting tile in this manner—three or four courses at a time—until you've reached the top of the splash or the windowsill. Remember to tap the tiles in with the beating block as you go.

WINDOW OPENINGS

As a rule, face cuts, or the cuts that are facing you, are installed first, then the trim pieces (bullnose), and finally, the cuts or pieces that cover the inside surfaces of the opening (see FIG. 3-44).

As you approach the windowsill, you'll notice (in most cases) that the last row of tiles will have to be cut in order to fit them under the trim pieces that will turn onto the sill itself. Lay a scrap piece of tile on the sill and position a piece of bullnose on the face of the sill so that the two pieces make a smooth transition from wall to sill. The distance from the bottom edge of the bullnose to the top of the last full course of tile will dictate the size of the cut (FIG. 3-45). Make enough of these cuts to go from one end of the sill to the other. Rub the cut edges with the rubbing stone. Just rub them enough to take the sharpness from the cut edge—don't wear them down. Now you can set the cuts, keeping them in line with the tiles already set.

In the bottom corners of the opening, you'll need inside corner pieces to turn the corner from horizontal to vertical (AM-4200, if you're using standard tile). You can miter the bullnose pieces if you have a saw. The corner pieces must be set in conjunction with a piece of bullnose going up the vertical edge of the opening. Hold a scrap piece of tile on the inside vertical surface and position a piece of bullnose so that the two make the transition smoothly. Now, set the inside corner piece so that it lines up with both the vertical and the horizontal pieces of bullnose (FIG. 3-46). You can now set the bullnose on the sill portion of the opening. The last piece will have to be cut, so set the other corner piece and then determine the size of the cut. Remember to rub the cut edge with the stone. If the cut is going to be small enough to appear unsightly, the bullnose

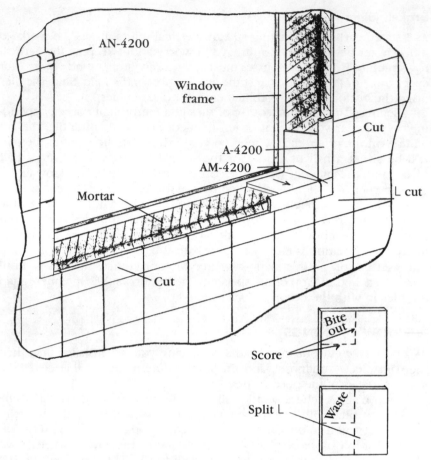

3-44 Detail of window area.

should be centered with a cut on both ends (FIGS. 3-47 to 3-49). Bullnose is cut on the cutting board by scoring as far around the radius portion as possible and positioning the "breaker" over the crown.

L cuts

Perhaps by now you've noticed that the wall tiles going around the bottom corners of the opening will have to be cut in the shape of an L in order to keep even courses of tile going up alongside the opening (FIG. 3-44).

If you have a saw, that's no problem, but seldom is there that luxury on a wall tile job. L cuts can be made on a cutting board by scoring the cut in both directions and then biting out the waste with the biters. It's not easy and patience is the key. After the tile has been scored, very small fragments are nipped off. You'll probably ruin several pieces of tile before you come up with an acceptable piece. The piece always seems to break on the very last bite.

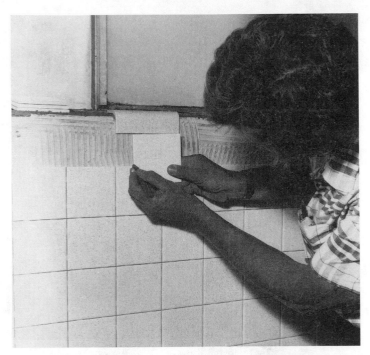

3-45 Marking the cuts under the sill.

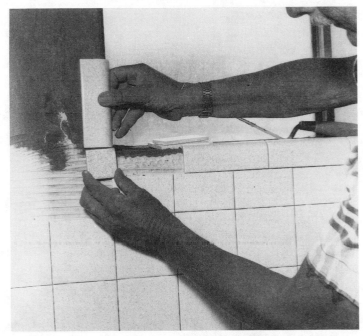

3-46 Installing the AM-4200 (inside corner).

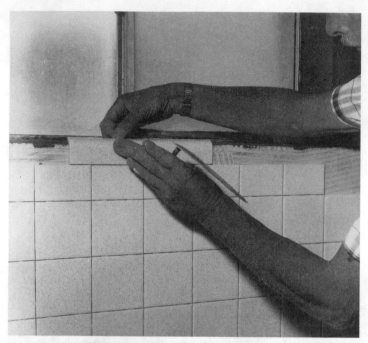

3-47. Install the A-4200 at the sill.

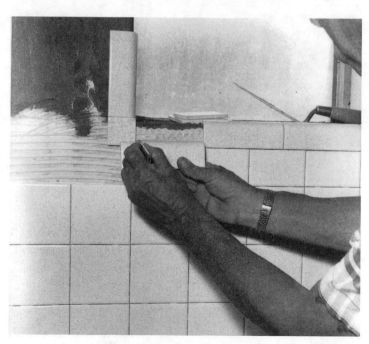

3-48 Marking A-4200 to be cut.

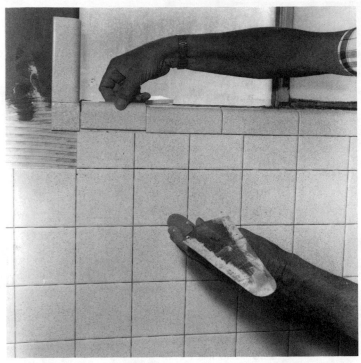

3-49 Installing the cut.

Splits

If you decide that a cut simply can't be made without a wet saw, and you've completely lost your composure, you might decide that a split cut is the answer. Splits are done in production work such as tract housing and commercial work. If done carefully, they're hardly noticed. If you can live with a split, and I can, do it. Save yourself a lot of frustration.

A split L cut is made by cutting completely across the tile in one direction and then cutting the piece that comes off in the other direction. When the two usable pieces are rejoined, you have your L, and if done carefully, the split between the two parts of the L is not readily noticeable. It's important to get the two sides of the L from the same piece of tile so that they go back together snugly (FIGS. 3-50 and 3-51).

Now that you have the trim pieces and the cuts under them set along the bottom edge of the opening, it's time to start up one side of the window. Cuts abutting the vertical trim pieces are made the same way as those under the sill. The vertical trim pieces must extend past the edge of the opening enough to meet the tiles that will be set on the inside surface, making a smooth transition around the turn (FIG. 3-44).

Position a piece of bullnose vertically above the inside corner piece and determine the size of the cuts. If you're using the broken joint method, you'll have cuts of two different sizes. After rubbing them, install

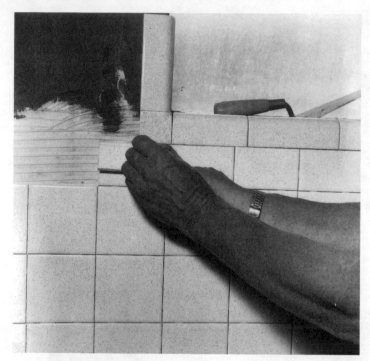

3-50 The split L cut.

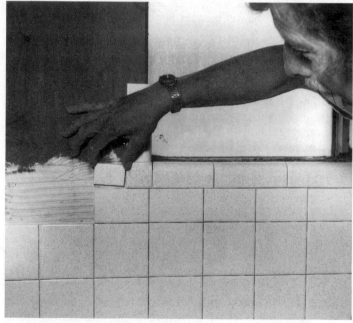

3-51 It's important to get both pieces from the same piece of tile.

the cuts and the field on one side of the opening, right up to the top of the splash. Use a level to ensure that everything is plumb. You can now install the bullnose. One of the trim pieces will have to be cut (FIG. 3-52).

3-52 Install the trim pieces at the side jamb.

If your splash goes beyond the top of the window opening, you'll have the same situation at the top as you had at the sill only in reverse. After you've run the tile and trim up on both sides of the opening, you can use a straightedge, cut to fit between the two sides, to temporarily hold the cuts in place. It takes only a minute or two for the cuts to stay put. You can then go ahead and run the field all the way to the top of the splash or to the ceiling. The top trim pieces are installed wall to wall across the back. The pieces on the end walls will later butt against them (FIGS. 3-53 to 3-55).

When all the tile, including the trim, has been installed on the wall itself, it's time to finish the inside surfaces of the window opening. Begin by tiling the sill, keeping in mind that it must slope in towards the tub so that water will run off of it. Then tile the header, and finally, the sides. The bottom tiles on the side jambs will have to be cut on a bias to accommodate the slope of the sill (FIGS. 3-56 and 3-57).

If the splash does not extend above the window opening, you'll need two outside corners to turn the trim back to the horizontal. If you're using standard wall tile, these are called *down angles* (AN-4200). You'll also need two of them for the corners on the end walls.

3-53 Place an A-4200 first.

3-54 Now place the outside corner (AN-4200).

3-55 Viola!

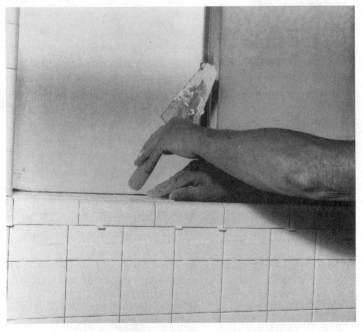

3-56 Set the pieces on the sill.

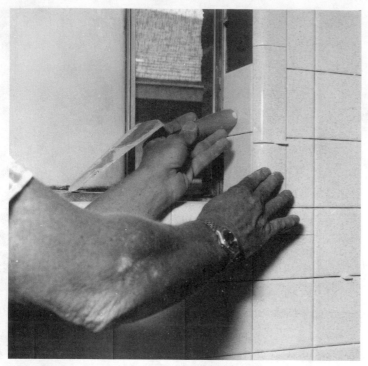

3-57 These pieces fit from the trim to the window sash.

FIXTURES

Ceramic soap dishes, towel bars, corner shelves, and any number of other items are referred to as fixtures, the most important of which is the soap dish. If you don't have a dish, you've got to rely on soap on a rope.

Just as there are standard wall tiles, there are also standard fixtures that fit vertically in the space of one course of 4¼ tile. They are semi-recessed and it's not necessary to remove the mortar from behind them, only the tile. Cuts still have to be made at the sides of the fixtures. The soap dish in a tub-shower combination is usually located in the center of the back wall one or two courses up from the top of the tub. If I might get off the track for a moment (you're thinking, he was off the track when he began writing), why not have two of them? You could have one in the standard location and another on the plumbing wall where it would be more convenient to use while taking a shower. After all, this is a custom job!

All you have to do is remove two tiles in the location you want to install the dish and put in equal cuts on both sides of the opening. The opening should measure 6 × 4¼ inches (FIG. 3-58). The dish itself, along with any other fixtures, will be installed during the grouting process, so don't worry about it now. Just leave the opening. You can pry out the tiles with a margin trowel or your tile setter's trowel. If you're setting the

3-58 Centering the soap dish opening.

tile with broken joints, you'll need a cut on only one side of the opening to center the dish. Should you elect to install an additional dish on the plumbing wall, a likely place would be between the showerhead and the valve towards the back wall. This is the location that receives the least shower spray and it's handy to reach while standing.

A towel bar is normally located on the end wall opposite the plumbing wall, as high as it is convenient to reach, usually two or three courses down from the top of a 5-foot splash. The standard towel bar bracket takes the space of half of a tile, so you can locate them where you like except that, if you might someday install a glass enclosure, you wouldn't want the outer bracket to be in the way.

Corner shelves are not standard, and advice on their installation should be obtained from the supplier. Corner shelves can be mounted in either corner of the splash, high enough to keep out of the shower spray. Custom fixtures are available in every size, shape, and color. Find out how to install them when you buy them.

END WALLS

After I finish tiling the back wall of a splash, I usually do the plumbing wall because it is the most difficult—you have to cut around the plumbing fixtures. Once you've completed the plumbing wall, the opposite wall will require no further instruction.

There are two important facts to be considered before you get started. The horizontal joints on the end wall must match those on the back wall. The front vertical row of tiles, going up the outside edge of the splash, must be set perfectly plumb. Or, if you're running the tiles on broken joints, the outside edges of the alternating full and half pieces must form a plumb line.

If you had to cut the bottoms off the first course of tiles on the back wall to level them, you'll have to cut the tiles on the bottom of at least one end wall, whichever is on the high end of the tub. To determine how much to cut off, hold your level horizontally across the end wall so that its top edge lines up with one of the horizontal joints on the back wall. Now, scratch a line in the mortar along the top edge of your level (FIG. 3-59). Bite off the bottoms of the first course as you did on the back wall. It might be possible to scratch your level line at the first joint above the tub but usually the tub spout pipe is in the way. The point is, of course, that the first course of tiles must be set level whether the tub is level or not, so nip off the bottom tiles accordingly. If the tub spout is low, you'll have to bite around it on the first course.

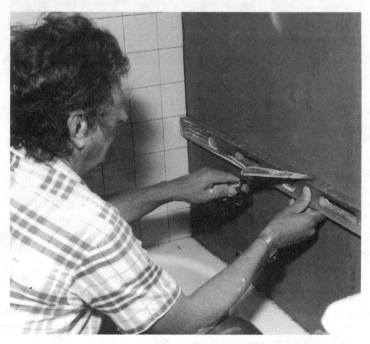

3-59 Scratching a level line in the mortar.

If you're going to use bullnose down the front of the tub, set the first tile with its outside edge even with the front of the tub. You can use your level. Rest it on the floor against the front of the tub to help you locate the first tile. The tiles are then set from the front of the tub to the back wall, with cuts being made in the corner. If you've extended the splash by more than the width of the bullnose, you'll set the first tile farther out from the front of the tub and run cuts down to the floor. Adjust the tile so that your trim fits properly on the edge of the mortar.

Because there are obstacles to be cut around almost immediately, it takes a while to get the first couple of courses installed, and the thin set might set before you get the tiles adjusted properly. If this happens, push your buttering trowel behind the tiles and remove them. Scrape off the backs and re-install them by buttering new thin set onto them. It can be frustrating, but after the first two courses are properly installed—level—with their horizontal joints lined up at the corner, it gets much easier.

Just when you've got things going smoothly, you'll run into the tub-shower valve, and if it's a single handle one protected with a plastic protector, the protector should be removed at this time. The opening in the mortar will guide you as you make the cuts around it, and the cuts should be made right up to the opening. You can try the trim plate in the opening from time to time as you're making the cuts to make sure it fits in against the tile snugly. If you're using the existing valve, you'll have only the trim plate and your memory to go by.

Then there are the valves with individual handles. There will be two or three valve stems protruding from the wall. Unless you're lucky, and I seldom am, you'll have to split some tiles to get around them. The tiles are split vertically, notches are made in both pieces, and then the two pieces are fit together around the stems. If this is done carefully, the split tiles won't be noticed after the wall is grouted. You could drill through the pieces, but nobody does this; splits are standard procedure. It's important to remember that the openings must provide for the use of tools inside them so that washers and seats can be changed without having to break out the tile (FIG. 3-60).

Spread thin set two or three courses up and set tile until you reach the valve. Don't spread the thin set all the way to the front edge of the wall where the trim will be installed. The trim pieces will be buttered on after the wall tile is set.

Begin setting tile at the outside edge of the wall. Hold your level vertically, along the edge, to help you get started. Remember, the front edge has to be plumb. If you're using the broken joint method, the half pieces must be rubbed on their cut edges. When you get to the valve, bite around it. If there are stems and you have to make splits, do it and get around the stems with your biters. This is going to take a while, so check for overglazing of the thin set. When you've gotten around the valve, you've got it made—until you get to the showerhead.

After you've conquered the valve, continue to set tile three or four courses at a time until you've reached the top. Getting around the shower arm is child's play. With my luck, I usually have to split a tile there too.

Trim pieces are installed beginning at the top, outside corner. They run horizontally to the corner at the back wall where a cut is usually required and from the top down to the floor where a cut is also made.

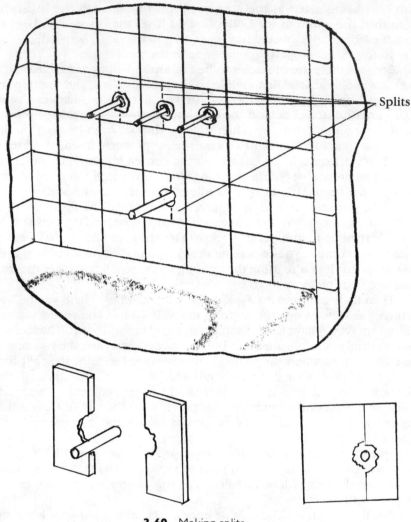

Splits

3-60 Making splits.

The cuts are always made where they won't be conspicuous, i. e., in the corners, at the floor, etc.

Once the back wall and the plumbing wall are completed, you won't need my help to tile the remaining end wall. Do remember to take out the tiles where the towel bar is to be installed, if you're installing one. If it's a standard one, you need to replace the tiles with halves.

After all the tiles and trim pieces have been installed, remove any shims you've installed and clean the entire surface of the splash with a sponge. Pay close attention to the joints. Make sure there is no thin set that might later protrude through the grout. I know—it's white, and the grout is probably going to be white, but the thin set contains sand, grout does not, and the sand will show through.

Now, thoroughly clean the tub itself. Cement products have a way of clinging to surfaces where they're not wanted. After you've cleaned up your mess, including your tools (and buckets), you're ready to grout or you can stand around, there's no hurry. Before you throw away the left-over thin set, butter a very thin coat on the backs of any fixtures you will install. The backs of most fixtures have been overglazed at the factory and the grout (which will hold them in), won't bond to them properly. A very light coat of thin set on their backs will make the installation absolutely bullet-proof.

GROUTING WALLS

Although the grouting process is by far the easiest of all, it could well be the most important. Grouting takes about one-tenth the time of the total project, and that's exactly how long it takes to ruin the whole thing if it's not done correctly and is allowed to set. I'm not trying to frighten you. You're a mud man or woman, and you can do anything, but take your time.

The grout we'll be using contains no sand. It is basically just cement. It is usually white but it can be pigmented if you desire a color. The colored grouts are premixed, and they're applied exactly like the white grout—you add water and stir.

Ask for ''dry wall grout'' at your tile supply. The white comes in 25-pound sacks. The colored grouts are usually available in smaller packages. It takes between 5 and 10 pounds to grout a tub splash.

In the old days, wall grout was applied with the hawk and trowel, but today, there's the rubber grout float, and I suggest you have one of these. Unless, of course, you feel you need more experience with the hawk and trowel.

Mixing grout

To mix grout, put a very small amount of water in the bottom of a clean bucket, about a pint. Now, add the dry grout in small amounts. Don't dump in the whole sack. The best descriptive word I can think of is creamy, not runny and not too stiff. The grout must have substance but you've got to be able to squeeze it into the joints with a float. (Don't seriously consider the use of a hawk and a trowel.) Mix small amounts because this is your first time, and you might not be as fast as you think you are—you can always make more if you need to. When you bring the grout into the bathroom, bring along a bucket of clean water with a clean sponge in it.

A professional might smear grout over the surface of the entire splash before beginning the washing process, but I think it best to concentrate on a smaller area. After you're familiar with the technique, larger areas can be contemplated.

Start with the end wall opposite the plumbing wall because it's relatively uncluttered. Start near the top of the wall and work your way down to the tub. When you're washing it off, you won't be dripping water on the work you've already completed.

Dip a gob of grout out of the bucket with the end of a float and push it on the wall, spreading it out as soon as it hits the wall. Hold the float at about a 30-degree angle to the wall and begin spreading it around, forcing it into the joints as you go. After you've spread a small area, say 4 or 5 square feet, turn the float at a steeper angle and scrape most of the grout from the surfaces of the tiles. Repeat the process.

Do the trim as you do the tiles, and push the grout all the way into the joints. You can get a little on the edge of the float and force it into the space between the bullnose and the bathroom wall. Don't push too hard on the trim pieces. The idea is to fill every space as you go so that you don't have to go back over an area. Don't exert a great deal of force, let the float do the work.

After you've completed the top half of the end wall, stop and begin washing it. By now, the grout should be firm in the joints and the surfaces of the tiles should be cloudy looking. If this is not the case, wait another two or three minutes before washing. Washing should commence within 10 to 15 minutes of the time you began smearing grout.

Wring the sponge so that it's not dripping and begin washing the surface with a wide, circular motion. Don't concentrate on any one area, but work the whole area you've grouted. Rinse the sponge frequently and the work will go faster. First, remove the grout from the surfaces of the tiles. Continue washing until this is accomplished (FIG. 3-61).

3-61 Washing the grout.

You can now concentrate on the joints. Keep the sponge moving. Don't wash one joint at a time, but all the joints. Use the same circular motion. You want to rub across the joints, not parallel to them. Otherwise, you might remove too much grout. I know it's not easy, but try to ignore the tiles themselves. As you wash, you'll notice the joints begin to straighten out, and the more you rub them, the narrower they'll become. When the joints are uniform and straight, it's time to stop washing. Wring the sponge tightly and go over the area again to remove some of the grout residue. You won't remove it all, but the wall will look cleaner. Stop—you're done.

Carefully examine the section of wall you've just completed. Check for wide, or fat, joints. Wipe across any you find with the sponge until they are uniform. If there are voids, fill them with grout and wash them. If grout has accumulated in the corners, get it out with your margin trowel and then wipe it again with the sponge. What you see is what you get. When the general appearance is pleasing, you're ready to go on to the next area.

Continue down the wall to the top of the tub. Push plenty of grout under the bottom course of tiles against the tub itself. After you've washed it, check the wall thoroughly for misses and irregular joints. Remember to concentrate on the the joints and not on the tiles themselves. Clean up the corners with the margin trowel. Corners should be square, not rounded. In general, make the appearance of your finished product as eye-appealing as possible. You won't get another chance.

You can move around the corner to the back wall and keep on going. You're a grouter now, and as long as you keep repeating the process in sequence, you're in good shape.

Elegant white octagons with black ''dots'' accentuate this breakfast room. The formal pattern carries through into the kitchen.

Look what diagonals can do to dress up an installation.

Glazed porcelain tiles. Don't get carried away!

Large wall tiles with matching inserts and contrasting molding do the trick in this bath.

Glazed Mexican tiles set diagonally to walls lend an informal air to any floor. Grout is portland cement mixed with masonry sand.

Imported clay tiles with feature strips and decorative edges.

Basic white with contrasting inlay.

Large, glazed Mexican tiles add a rustic touch to this modern den.

The ultimate bath. Glazed Mexican tiles contribute to the ''atrium'' look of the room.

Chapter **11**

Finishing up

*T*his chapter will not only cover how to install soap dishes and towel bars, but how to seal the tile installation to make it easier to keep clean. You may also want to install a glass enclosure or a heavy-duty grab bar, and you'll need to know how to drill through the tiles. And finally, we'll talk about other types of tile that might be considered for use on the tub splash, or any other wall for that matter.

INSTALLING FIXTURES

The fixtures on any given wall can be installed after it has been grouted and washed or once the entire splash has been grouted. It really doesn't matter. To install a ceramic fixture, load the back of it with grout, and push it into the opening you've provided for it. Push it all the way in and hold it for a moment—30 seconds or so. Remove the excess grout from around it with your finger or your margin trowel. Let the grout set for 10 minutes. (See FIGS. 3-62 through 3-64.)

Wash around the fixture with a sponge until all of the excess grout is removed and you're satisfied with its appearance. It's a good idea to hold the fixture with one hand while washing with the other. You won't be apt to inadvertently knock it loose. That's all there is to it! One more thing though. When installing a towel bar, don't install both brackets without the bar in between them (FIG. 3-65). I know it sounds stupid but it can happen. The plastic bar can be cut to length with a hack saw or a carpenter's saw.

When the grout job has been completed, allow the splash to dry for an hour and then wipe the surface with a clean, dry cloth. You can sprinkle a few drops of Old English lemon oil on the cloth to help contain the dust. Ready for a shower? Not in this tub. Let it set for a day or two before using it, and if you want to seal it with masonry sealer, you'll have to wait even longer.

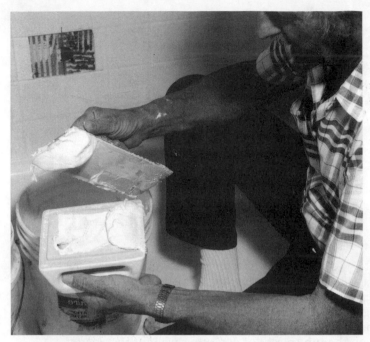

3-62 Installing the soap dish. Thin set is spread on the back of the fixture before the grout is applied.

3-63 Push the dish all the way in.

3-64 Remove excess grout from the soap dish.

3-65 Make sure you've installed the rod before you install the final bracket.

SEALERS

One of the questions asked frequently is, how do I keep the grout in my shower clean? The answer usually boils down to elbow grease, but if the grout and tiles are sealed with a penetrating masonry sealer, you're ahead of the game. Besides soap scum, the most common cause of discoloration in grout is mildew, which is caused by moisture in the grout. If that moisture can be excluded from the grout joints, mold and mildew won't be able to take root.

There are several types of sealers available, some water-based, some mineral-based. Being an old-fashioned tile setter, I like the mineral-base products—the ones that smell bad. The best one I've found is penetrating silicone sealer, which is sold at most tile supply stores as well as at home centers and masonry supplies. It's easy to use—just follow the directions on the container. Wipe it on with a cloth or a sponge and let it saturate the joints, then remove the excess with a dry cloth. Buy the smallest container possible; it takes only a little to do the job.

Before you can seal a splash, however, you must allow at least a week for the splash to dry out, which means you're not going to use it for a week. You have to make sure all the moisture in the mortar has evaporated, otherwise the sealer will cloud and streak. I do recommend that you seal your splash. It'll save wear and tear on the maid. (See FIG. 3-66.)

3-66 Ready for a shower? Not in this tub.

DRILLING THROUGH TILE

Shower enclosures, metal grab bars, and other metal fixtures require that holes be drilled through the tile and substrate. The size of the holes depends on the size of the screws and the anchors to be used. I won't get into installation because again, this is the province of plumbers, but I'll give you a few pointers on drilling.

Wait two or three days before drilling any holes so that the substrate has time to harden. With a small center punch or a large nail and a hammer, make a very small "ding" in the tile glaze. This prevents the drill from traveling. It's not necessary to use a great deal of force, wall tiles are generally soft. Just tap the nail or punch until you've made a small pit in the glaze.

Use a masonry bit, obtainable at any hardware store, in an electric drill. Do not use a hammer drill. Holding the drill steady, drill straight into the tile all the way through the mortar. The screw anchor can now be tapped in gently with a hammer.

Shower curtain rods

I prefer the type of shower curtain rod that requires no holes be drilled. The rod is held in place by compression and friction. Why drill holes if you don't have to? Of course, if you enjoy drilling holes, just make sure they're drilled at the same height at each end of the tub splash. The rods must be installed level.

STUD WALLS

Suppose the opposite side of a wall you've tiled is in a bedroom and you want to install book shelves on that wall. The worst thing you could do is drive nails into the studs, vibrating the wall and the tile installation on the other side. The preferred method is to use screws. Tile installations of the type we've discussed are extremely strong, but they will crack before they bend. Don't take any chances. On the other hand, driving a small brad to hang a picture is not a problem provided the substrate has been allowed to cure.

OTHER TYPES OF TILE

As I said earlier, any type of tile can be set on a wall, and that includes tub splashes. I've installed large floor tiles in showers and tub surrounds on numerous occasions, as well as a row of pool tiles to spice up a drab installation. But the second most common tile used in showers is made from porcelain. Porcelain tiles are usually mounted on sheets and the whole sheet is set intact.

Tiles on sheets

It's best to set sheets on dry mortar. The tile is dense and doesn't absorb much moisture. Therefore, it takes forever for them to set up and stop moving around after they've been set. The dry mortar absorbs some of the moisture, allowing the thin set to take hold faster.

Another consideration is that these tiles don't have spacer lugs, and as soon as the backing gets wet, it's hard to move the sheet. So, the tiles have to be supported by some other means. Don't laugh—I usually nail them up.

It's best to figure out your layout and start at the top of the wall. The sheets are "hung" level across the top of the wall with small nails driven into the dry mortar. The nails can be driven between the first and second course of tiles on the sheet with maybe a few poked in farther down the sheet to give it a little stability. Subsequent sheets are then hung under the first course of sheets until the tub is reached.

If the mortar is hard, drive the nails only into it and not clear into the sheetrock. I sometimes tape the lower sheets to the ones above them with masking tape. It just depends on what's on hand. No matter, a few nails should be used on subsequent sheets so that the entire weight of a vertical row is not on the one upper sheet.

Of course, if you're starting from the top, it's important to know that the last sheets are going to fit above the tub, so do your arithmetic before you start setting tile. You can run a vertical row of sheets from the top down to the tub to get your range, then go back to the top and work down. Use your level to get the vertical row plumb (FIG. 3-67).

When cuts are needed, tiles must be removed from the sheets where they are cut on a cutting board like wall tiles and installed individually. Masking tape works great for holding the cuts in place while they set.

Grouting is best accomplished with a rubber float used in conjunction with a hawk. Porcelain tiles are almost always grouted with sanded grout, which doesn't cling to the float like unsanded grout. A good bit of grout is dropped during the process and it's nice to have the hawk against the wall to catch it with. Get a small amount of grout on the hawk and flatten it with the float. Turn the hawk toward you and scoop off the grout with the edge of the float. Because the tiles don't absorb much moisture, it takes longer for the grout to set in the joints. Wait about 15 or 20 minutes before washing the grout.

Small ceramic tiles are also sometimes mounted on sheets, which are installed in the same manner as porcelain tiles. If the joints are $1/8$ of an inch or less, they can be grouted with unsanded grout—the same as wall tiles. If the joints are wider than about $1/8$ an inch, use sanded grout.

You might encounter $4^{1}/4$ wall tiles in sheets. The brainchild of a large U.S. manufacturer of tile, $4^{1}/4$ tiles were supposed to revolutionize the industry. The tiles are mounted in 4×4 tile sheets, 17 inches square, which makes them cumbersome to handle. There are other disadvantages. The tiles must be removed from the sheets to cut them. If your tub is not level, you'll be disassembling sheets just to get started and, as mentioned in chapter 11, tiles are not perfect and it takes some adjustment to get them set straight. Moving individual tiles bonded together on sheets is not possible. Last, they're expensive. Someone has to pay for the added cost of mounting them. Who? I'll give you three guesses.

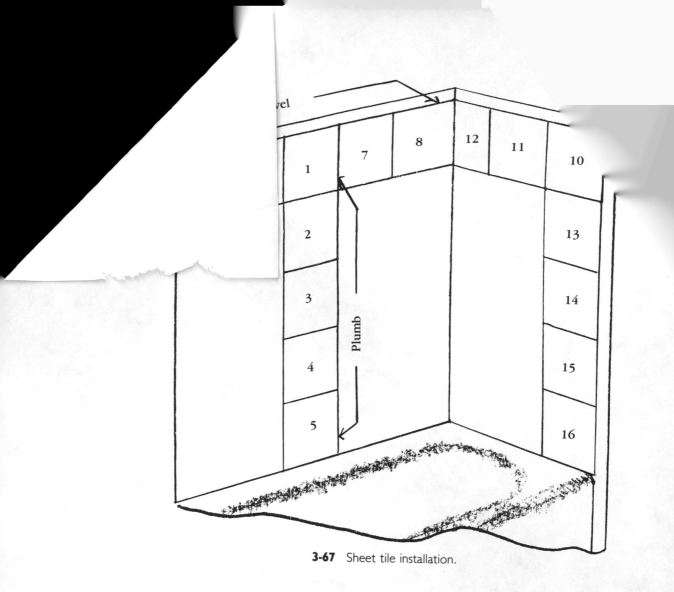

3-67 Sheet tile installation.

Floor tiles

Floor tiles can also be used on walls. Plastic spacers, which are inserted after each course, are available from tile suppliers. Because most floor tiles are slightly irregular in size and shape, a little adjusting will have to be done on the way up the wall. Just keep the rows plumb and level.

When larger pieces of tile are used, tiles are drilled instead of split cut. Hole saws, which attach to an electric drill, are usually available at masonry and tile supplies.

In most cases, matching trim pieces are not available for floor tiles. You can use standard wall tile trims and just coordinate the colors. Use your imagination. Floor tiles are also grouted with sanded grout, so you'll have to get out the old hawk.

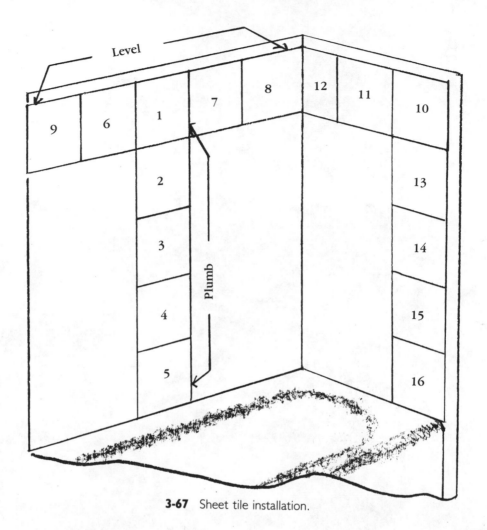

3-67 Sheet tile installation.

Floor tiles

Floor tiles can also be used on walls. Plastic spacers, which are inserted after each course, are available from tile suppliers. Because most floor tiles are slightly irregular in size and shape, a little adjusting will have to be done on the way up the wall. Just keep the rows plumb and level.

When larger pieces of tile are used, tiles are drilled instead of split cut. Hole saws, which attach to an electric drill, are usually available at masonry and tile supplies.

In most cases, matching trim pieces are not available for floor tiles. You can use standard wall tile trims and just coordinate the colors. Use your imagination. Floor tiles are also grouted with sanded grout, so you'll have to get out the old hawk.

Chapter **12**

Setting other walls

*I*n acquainting you with the possibilities of tiling walls in other areas, I don't want you to feel limited by my suggestions. I come up with new ideas almost every day, and you will too. In fact, this chapter contains just a few suggestions. The decorating possibilities of ceramic tile are endless, and setting tile in any room of your house is no more difficult than tiling a tub splash. In fact, it is much easier. The same basic principles apply—centering, setting the tiles level and plumb, and equalizing cuts.

WAINSCOTS

Tiled surfaces that go partially up a wall are called *wainscots*. In this respect, I suppose a tub surround would fit into this category. The only thing to remember about wainscots is that the top course of tile is always full—no cuts at the top. It is also visually impressive if the bottom tiles are also full pieces, but this is not always possible. A wainscot is sometimes part of a tub splash and the courses must line up with it. If the bathroom floor is to be tiled, shoe base, or a cove piece, is often used at the bottom of the wainscot to make a rounded transition to the floor. The cuts are then made immediately above the base with the cut edge turned down.

When tiling a wainscot that is a continuation of a tub splash, do the splash first, leaving off the trim pieces at the splash-wainscot juncture. Then do the wainscot. Line up the tiles with those on the splash, and make your cuts at the floor. Install the remaining trim pieces last (FIG. 3-68).

WALLS IN OTHER AREAS OF THE HOME

Sheetrock walls have been the standard in American homes for the past 40 or 50 years, and they hold up well as long as they don't get wet.

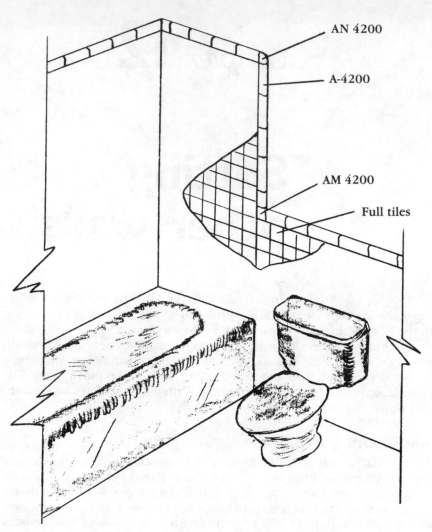

AN 4200

A-4200

AM 4200

Full tiles

3-68 This wainscot lines up with the tub splash.

Because the walls in most rooms around the home are not likely to get wet, sheetrock is an adequate substrate for ceramic tile. Of course, in the old days, all ceramic tiles were installed over masonry, but there's really very little reason to do so today. The walls behind the countertops in a kitchen, for example, are seldom wet, and if they are, they're wiped off almost immediately. So if the walls are straight, I don't think it's necessary to do a mud job on them. I'm not that old-fashioned. On the other hand, if the walls are in close proximity to a spa or in an area where high humidity is common, such as a steam room or laundry room, the tiles should definitely be installed over a masonry substrate—if not mud, cement backer board.

DESIGNING WALLS AND WAINSCOTS

When designing walls and wainscots, the sky is the limit, but certain consideration must be given to basic design and current trends. You are the designer, and it's your house—now—but you might someday want to put it on the market, sell the old homestead. In this case, any alterations you make now must make the house more, not less, desirable to a prospective buyer.

Remember, ceramic tile is somewhat permanent; it's not easily removed. I'm not a designer, but I've learned that too much color and patterns that are too busy, tend to get on one's nerves as the years go by. And trends change almost yearly. On the other hand, you're the person who matters. So after giving it careful thought, do it. The only conclusion I've drawn through long years of experience is that: if the homeowner likes it, it's good. If the homeowner doesn't like it, it's very, very bad.

Mirrors and tile go very well together. Think about a wall in the living room or den with plate glass mirrors separated by rows of ceramic tiles. Because you're the designer and builder, the arrangement can be made modular, meaning no cuts will be needed. Also, separating mirror panels can greatly decrease the cost of a mirrored wall. If the panels don't have to fit from floor to ceiling, stock mirrors can be purchased and you can install them yourself. The tiles themselves can be put up with mastic or installed with the same adhesive used to put up the mirrors. Trim pieces are available for the edge of the wall or for framing the mirrors themselves. This technique also works well on a square column. The tile makes the corners, and narrow mirror panels are inserted between them.

Sun rooms (or greenhouse rooms in Yankee Land) and game rooms lend themselves to ceramic tile wainscots. Tiles can go around the window, including the sills. Sills should be done with mortar, however, because the condensation on windows is a consideration in every climate. In game rooms, the wainscot could go around the entire room.

Usually, a ceramic tile wainscot begins at the floor. The tile is set up to the desired height, and then capped with a trim piece or a wood molding such as a chair rail. The main consideration is getting started straight and level. The high and low points in the floor must be identified, and the first row of tiles is either cut or "coped" to fit over the irregularities in the floor or raised above the highest point of the floor, provided it's not too far out of level. Carpeting can always cover the gap.

Going over the floor with a level is one way to determine high or low spots, but not the best way. Hold the level at any height, and by extending it from one end of the wall to the other, draw a line across the wall. By measuring down from the line to the floor, the differences will become readily apparent. Of course, the line should be drawn where it'll be hidden by the tile. If the tiles must be cut at the bottom of the wall to accommodate irregularities in the floor, it's best to cut about 1/2 inch off so that all the cuts can be made on a cutting board. Biting off enough tiles to go from one end of a room to the other gets tiresome and the little extra you cut off with the cutter won't be noticeable.

This is where mastic comes into play. Tiles set in mastic tend to stay put, whereas, with thin set, they'll slump if not supported. Therefore, if you use mastic, you can set the entire field, and then put the cuts in under it, trimming them off as needed.

You could even draw a level line at the top of the proposed field, set the top course along it, and then install the remaining tiles from the top down. The cuts are then made to fit at the floor. You could also draw a line half way between the wainscot and the floor, setting the tiles level at that point. The field down to the floor and up to the top edge would then be filled in.

When installing a wainscot on a long wall, it's best to start in the middle and work to both ends. It's easier to correct minor errors, such as being out of level and out of plumb, if the distance is half as long as the entire wall. Tiles installed in mastic can be moved around for a period of time, and they'll still stay where you put them.

MURALS

Most domestic tile manufacturers produce murals. They come in sets, and installation directions are usually included in the package. Ask to see the catalogs at your tile supply store. Not only are stock murals available, but many companies produce custom-made ones made to specification. These are works of art, and they're priced accordingly. In addition, some local artists create art work on existing wall tiles. Once the tiles are completed, they are re-fired.

Remember that layout is the all important factor. Never install the first piece of tile without knowing where the final piece is going to be placed. And take your time. Time spent contemplating a project is not wasted; it is necessary and vital.

Part 4

CERAMIC TILE COUNTERS

What could be more durable and long-lasting than tile? And what could possibly be as elegant and appealing? Decorating trends come and go, but through the years, one medium has endured. A wholesome product formed in nature and brought to fruition by the hand of man—ceramic tile—the "real thing."

Plastic laminates are durable to a degree and there is almost an infinite number of styles and colors to choose from, but let's face it, they look like plastic. They don't have that certain glow. What of the new solid plastics? They are impressive and expensive, but don't they appear a bit commercial?

Decades ago in this country and others, ceramic tile kitchen and bathroom counters appeared in only the best homes. The owners knew what they wanted and were able to pay for it. The cost of labor was expensive and still is. Inch for inch, a ceramic tile counter is one of the most expensive projects done by professional tile setters to this day.

The price of tile varies by style and color, but the cost of labor is certainly the biggest factor to consider. You can have your entire kitchen floor done in ceramic tile for what it costs to have the counters done, sometimes less. On average, labor and overhead contribute about 75 percent to the cost of having kitchen counters tiled. Then there is usually some rough carpentry involved—some plumbing work—more labor. But this is where the home do-it-yourselfer comes in. A person who otherwise might not be able to afford the work, who is willing to supply the labor and overhead, will find the project affordable indeed.

If you consider the project on a material basis only, it becomes more and more attractive. The labor involved is certainly not easy, but it is within the grasp of the average do-it-yourselfer. The best descriptive word I can think of is tedious. Very little tile is set without having to make cuts, and many of the pieces are shapes, which are even harder to cut and set. And then, just when you really get going, along comes a sink or a stove top or some other obstruction to be cut around. The back splash is even worse. Electrical outlets, window sills, and in older homes, wall-mounted faucets connive to get in our way. It truly never ends!

Is it all worth the trouble? You bet! And if I haven't talked you out of it, let's get going.

Chapter **13**

Countertop tiles

*T*here are no special tiles made specifically for countertops but many varieties are suitable and attractive. In the case of a kitchen counter, durability has to head the list of desirable characteristics. In this sense, floor tiles certainly qualify. Porcelain tiles, whether they are mosaics or larger pieces, are an excellent choice. Hard-glazed ceramic wall tiles are also an option.

Unfortunately, standard wall tile and trim pieces have been the norm for kitchen countertops throughout the years. In my opinion, most wall tiles are not suitable for the drain board. The bisques are not dense enough to support the glaze in case of dropped utensils or other bumps that occur in the kitchen on a daily basis. And then there is the worry of abrasion of the glaze itself.

I've seen counters done 50 or 60 years ago with porcelain mosaics that are still in good shape. The grout might be discolored and even missing in places, but the tiles are still pristine. On the other hand, I've seen counters done only 10 years ago with wall tile that have to be torn out and re-done—very little glaze remains on the surfaces of the tiles. Of course, some people are more careful than others, but why have to worry about it?

There are, however, wall tiles with fairly tough, resilient glazes. The advantage of using this type of tile is that trim shapes are always available. A-8262, for example, forms a smooth rounded edge and takes care of both the vertical surface and the top edge without a grout joint. The alternative is using two pieces to form this juncture. Or, you can trim the edge with wood.

There is also the option of using more durable tiles on the surface and A-8262 in a complementary color for the edge. This method produces an appealing contrast of color and surface texture. Provision must be made for the difference in thickness between the two different types of tile, however, but this can normally be accomplished if contemplated ahead of time.

NOTE: Do not incorporate the use of A-8262 into your design if you won't have access to a tile saw. The pieces can't be cut on a cutting board, and trying to bite them off with nippers leaves them in a shambles.

Handmade clay tiles possess a certain eye-appeal. Their irregular shape lends a rustic air to the decorating scheme and the choice of color and pattern is unlimited, but many of them are much too soft if durability and longevity are considerations.

If you live in a household where the kitchen is seldom used, a show place so to speak, durability won't be a consideration. But let's face it, most of us aren't in that enviable situation. Durability is less important in the bathroom. Vanity tops are used much less than kitchen countertops. You spend a few minutes in the bathroom, but most people absolutely live in the kitchen. Wall tile is a good choice in the bath because it can match the tile used in the shower area and not be subjected to the constant wear and tear of a kitchen counter. But let's get back to the kitchen.

DESIGN

As I said in earlier chapters, my views on basic design are not shared by everyone, nor should they be. You are the final authority on what goes into your kitchen. My only qualifications are that I've been in many kitchens, worked with a number of interior designers, professional and amateur, and installed tile on more than one drain board. Therefore, I'll offer you just a few words of advice: Don't overdo it. The counter is going to out-last curtains, wallpaper, and paint, so try to control yourself!

BORDERS

Borders can be plain tile in a contrasting color or decorated in any number of ways. They can be tiles of the same color with different textures. Borders can be set around the perimeter of a countertop, on the back splash, or both. Borders can be more than one row of tiles, or they can be alternating pieces of different colors. More than one border, such as stripes, can be incorporated into the design. The only consideration is a technical one—the size and thickness of the pieces used to form the border. The work goes much easier if border pieces are the same size as the tiles used in the field.

INSERTS (DECO'S)

Decorated tiles made from the same bisque as the field tiles are available. If not, most good tile suppliers contract with artists to decorate stock tiles with custom designs. The tiles are then re-fired. The service can be expensive but worth investigating. Deco's made from other bisques can also be used if size and shape permit. Sculpted tiles in bas-relief are sometimes used as inserts, and groups of smaller tiles can take the place of a field tile.

FEATURE STRIPS

A feature strip, also called a liner, is an item from the past that is currently being revived. Remember when wall tile always appeared with contrasting trim? (I'm giving away my age.) There were green tiles with maroon trim, yellow and black, pink and gray, and one of my favorites, ugly gray tile with equally ugly black trim.

Somewhere in the installation was usually a strip of contrasting tile about 1/2 inch wide—the feature strip. It could be found toward the top of the kitchen splash, around the tub enclosure, or a couple of courses down from the top of the bathroom wainscot. Well, guess what? It's back, only now there are more feature strips to choose from, ranging in width from 1/2 inch to 1 or 2 inches. I just thought you might be interested.

CONTRASTING TRIM

As I've mentioned, trim pieces don't necessarily have to be the same color or texture as the field tiles. The same trim, however, should be used throughout the project. Continuity must be maintained.

DIAGONALS

Square tiles can be set diagonally to a splash or diagonally on the splash. It involves more cutting but it's certainly an option. You're going to have to do your shopping. If you live in or near a large city, you'll find numerous tile showrooms to choose from. If you live in a rural area, I suggest you make a trip to the city. We're fortunate in Houston. We are one of the major import points in the country for tile from Europe, South America, Mexico, and the Far East. In smaller communities, tile is usually sold by carpet and flooring companies, and the variety is limited.

I might also mention that there is a general misconception about tiles mounted on sheets and the facility of their installation. Because more tiles are set at the same time, shouldn't the work go faster? Not at all, especially in the kitchen. There are very few areas where full sheets can be installed on a back splash. More often, tiles must be removed from the sheets to accommodate electrical outlets and switches. When any cutting is to be done, more cuts are needed, and the pieces must be removed from the sheet. In this respect, sheets are not a boon, they're a pain.

ESTIMATING MATERIAL

Because no two projects are alike, I can't do the estimating for you, I can only tell you how to go about it. First, if the counter and splash are to be predominately the same tile, figure (in square feet) the area to be covered. It helps to divide the project into smaller rectangles and figure their areas. Total the areas of all the rectangles. I go back and measure in the opposite direction, re-figure the area, and try to come up with the same total. Do not deduct for the space the trim pieces will occupy. The extra tile ordered will make up for cutting and other waste. Besides, I'd rather have a few too many tiles than too few.

It helps if you treat the counter and the splash as separate projects when considering trim. In many cases, the trims on the counter will be different in shape from those on the splash. A simple check list might help:

Outside corners   Start at one end of the counter and work to the other. Each open end will require at least one corner. Eating bars might require two.

Inside corners   Required in Ls, or Us, usually on the splash, are only at the window opening.

Straight trims   Measure the perimeter of the counter twice, from both directions. Standard wall tile trims are sold by the piece. Sheet-mounted trims (stretchers) are usually sold by the linear foot. Do not deduct for the corners. You need a few spare pieces of trim. Now, do the same at the splash. Don't forget the windowsill. It's advisable to have spare trim left over when the project is complete. The counter edge pieces are the most susceptible to future damage.

Borders and inserts   Figure the total number of pieces and convert them to square feet (144 square inches). Add two or three pieces for spares. Decorative tiles (deco's) are sold by the piece. I don't buy any spares because they're too expensive. Deduct the area they will cover (in square feet) from the amount of field tile you'll be ordering.

Feature strips (liners)   Measure the length and add two pieces. They are sold by the piece.

Cement products   Tile suppliers can assist you in ordering cement products. They'll know what you need by the amount of tile you purchase and the nature of the project.

Be sure to purchase plastic spacers, shims (wedges), etc., and if you haven't read chapter 2 on tools, you need to do so now. Make sure that you have everything you need before you begin the job.

Chapter **14**

Countertop surfaces

*I*f you've been reading along in the previous chapters, you're no doubt aware that I am a mud man, and mud men never give up (or shut up), and certainly not in the kitchen. Without a doubt, lath and mortar form the best substrate for ceramic tile counters, and we'll go through a mud project step by step, but there are other surfaces, though less desirable, that are also suitable.

PLASTIC LAMINATE

Ceramic tile can be applied directly to laminate countertops provided they are in good shape and well bonded. Mastics are available that will do the job. I recommend using a mineral-base adhesive, not a water-based or latex-based adhesive. Mineral-based mastics seem to form a harder bond and they're not as susceptible to water. A kitchen or bathroom counter must be considered a semi-wet area. It's not flooded with water as a tub surround is but it's going to get wet from time to time.

Deflection is a consideration with this type of installation. If you entertain frequently and the party always seems to end up in the kitchen, before you know it, someone will decide to jump up and sit on the counter. If that person is petite, it might not cause a problem. So, should you only give parties for petite people? A better idea would be to do what you can to shore up the counter or choose some other method of installation.

Laminate must be thoroughly cleaned and degreased before attempting to apply mastic. An abrasive detergent should be used liberally and the surface then thoroughly rinsed. After it's dry, sand the laminate with medium-grit sandpaper to rough it up. This will form a "tooth" that enables the adhesive to form a better bond to the surface. Don't forget to wipe or vacuum up the dust.

PLYWOOD

Exterior grade plywood is also an adequate substrate for ceramic tile on a counter. If you're replacing the top or building new countertops, grade AD plywood with exterior glue should be used. Don't consider anything less than 3/4-inch plywood, and an excellent installation can be accomplished using two layers of plywood, glued and screwed together. In this case, the under sheet would not have to be exterior grade.

Don't consider using interior grade plywood directly under the tile—don't even think about it! Even if water never contacts the counter, moisture will still get into the wood in the form of condensation. Spend a little more money and get something that'll last much longer.

The best adhesive to use over plywood is multipurpose thin set mortar. Thin set is impervious to moisture and because it contains latex, it is somewhat water-resistant.

PARTICLE BOARD

What about particle board? Don't try it. It can swell to twice its thickness when it gets damp.

CEMENT BACKER BOARD

Next to lath and mortar, cement backer board is probably the best possible substrate for counters. It must be backed by at least 3/4-inch-thick plywood (your existing top), because it is not rigid enough to support itself. If you can get the cement board made in 4-×-8-foot sheets, you'll be ahead of the game. You'll have fewer joints, meaning better continuity. Unfortunately, the larger sheets are generally not stocked and will probably have to be special-ordered. Also available are 3-×-5-foot sheets, and if forethought is used, there's little waste.

Cement board can be glued as well as nailed to an existing countertop, and I recommend doing both. Nails alone have a way of working loose as the years go by. Use 1 1/2-inch galvanized roofing nails. The best adhesive to use when setting tile over cement backer board is thin set mortar. On countertops, I use white thin set, which is formulated for walls. The open time is a bit longer and it's just as strong as the gray type.

A magazine article I once read suggested the use of wall tile mastic over cement backer board. To me, this seems folly. You've got a cement-based substrate, which is essentially impervious to moisture, and ceramic tile, which is not adversely affected by water. Why put a layer of synthetic material between the two? Mastics do not hold up under wet conditions for extended periods of time. I use mastics when I feel thin set won't do the job, such as over plastic laminate, for example.

WAFER BOARD

Wafer board, or chip board, is formed with exterior glue and is becoming popular as an exterior sheathing in construction, mainly because of its price. It's much cheaper than exterior grade plywood. The word "cheaper" always scares me a little, however. I don't know if it's adequate for use directly beneath ceramic tile and I think I'll let someone else put it to the test.

DIMENSION LUMBER

Wood boards are not an acceptable substrate for ceramic tile for two reasons: They expand and shrink depending on the moisture content and they provide no continuity.

EXISTING TILE TOPS

The first order of business for existing tile tops is to get out the hammer and chisel, and maybe the wrecking bar. You're in the demolition business again. I've never found a way of going over existing tile countertops and making them look like new. The problem isn't so much getting the new tiles to adhere, but that the old trim gets in the way of the new. It's less frustrating to tear out the old installation and re-do the whole thing in the long run.

Try not to damage the cabinets, and protect the floor. If the existing tile is simply glued to the top, it's easier to remove the entire top and replace it with new plywood than to remove the tiles only. In older installations, the sink is tiled into the top. This is a good time to consider replacing the sink. The newer ones mount on top of the tile.

CEMENT MORTAR

And then there is cement mortar—good old mud. There's nothing like it in the whole world. For as long as countertops have been done in tile, cement mortar has been used as the foundation. Three-quarters of an inch of mortar, reinforced with metal lath or chicken wire (poultry netting), makes the installation absolutely unshakable. An inch of mortar is even better.

The overlapped reinforcing material forms a continuous armature with no joints to pull apart, and the entire installation, tile and substrate, is impervious to water. Most important, your heaviest party guest can do push-ups on the counter without so much as causing it to quiver. The mud method is time-consuming, labor-intensive, messy—it is all of these things—but it is the best.

In years past, tile setters always applied mud to everything they set tile to, but in the case of a kitchen back splash, I don't think this is necessary. If the sheetrock or plaster is in good shape and is smooth and fair, tile can be set right over it. It's not going to get wet, and if it does, it's usually wiped off immediately. Of course, a better installation would be cement board nailed over the sheetrock and into the studs.

In this chapter, our project will consist of applying mortar over the countertops and tiling the splash over an added layer of sheetrock.

I would be remiss if I didn't discuss the time factor involved. Don't expect to start in the morning and have the project completed by supper.

Regardless of the method chosen, the work will go on for, at the very least, two days, and then the grout will have to dry before the counter can be used. The necessary plumbing and carpentry work must also be considered. Visualize how long it'll take to complete your project and then double the time estimate. If it's done sooner, you'll be pleasantly surprised. If it's not, you won't be disappointed.

PREPARING THE ROUGH TOP

All you need to get going is a solid foundation to build your substrate on. The process is very similar to floating a wood floor, which is discussed in Part 2. This foundation, or *rough top*, can be wood boards, plywood, or wafer board. It can even be your existing plastic laminate countertop. It should, however, be $3/4$ of an inch thick to provide stability until the mortar cures.

If you're installing new cabinets or replacing the tops on the existing ones, the rough top can be nailed directly to them. If you'll be using sink

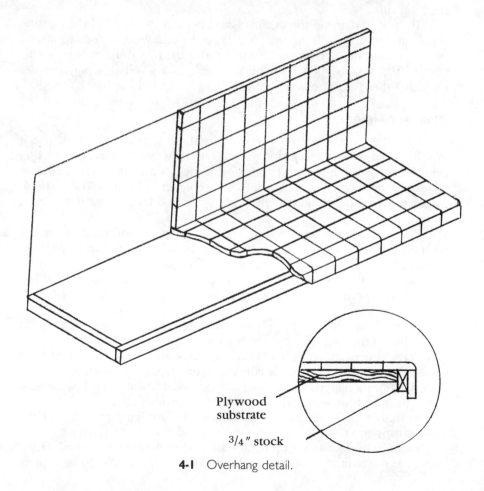

Plywood
substrate

$3/4''$ stock

4-1 Overhang detail.

rail (A-8262), cut the material flush with the front of the cabinet face frames for the edge trim. Sink rail protrudes about $3/8$ to $1/2$ inch from the cabinet face. If more overhang is desired, let the rough top protrude a $1/4$ inch or so. If you're going to be using a surface-type cap for the trim, you'll need an overhang that can be added to the edge. (See FIG. 4-1.)

When installing cabinets or new countertops, you must consider clearances for built-in appliances such as dishwashers, compactors, and ice makers. The cabinets can either be shimmed up at the floor or you can build up the cabinets under the countertops. You don't want to end up having to make a notch so the dishwasher door will open. Also, if you decide to later install a ceramic tile floor in the kitchen, now is the time to make provision for it. A little extra height at the counter won't make any difference. If you're going to use the mud method on the counters, allow about $3/4$ of an inch for mortar. Clearances for standard appliances are provided in FIG. 4-2.

If your present countertops are plastic laminate, and you're going to use the mud method, you'll have to cut the overhang flush with the cabinet face frames. This can be done with a circular saw equipped with a carbide-tipped blade. If you have the molded (rounded) edged counters, the

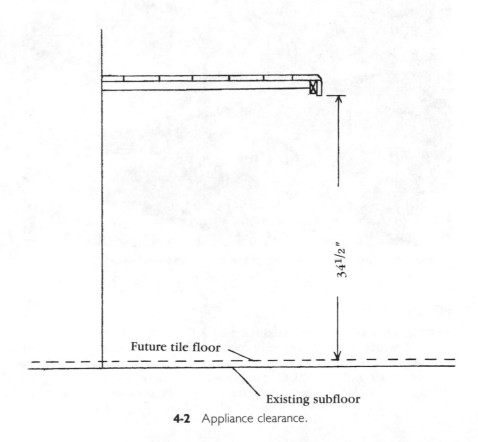

4-2 Appliance clearance.

overhang will be removed regardless of what method you use. Then, if you're simply planning to glue the tile directly to the top, you can install a new square edge piece (FIG. 4-1).

MOISTURE BARRIERS

Moisture barriers are applied to all wood rough tops. If you're going over plastic laminate, you won't need a moisture barrier because the laminate is waterproof. Use four-mil poly (sheet plastic) or 15-pound felt (tar paper). Lay it over the rough top before installing the lath. Overlap the pieces by 2 or 3 inches. Not only does the moisture barrier protect the wood rough top, it prevents the mortar from dehydrating too quickly. The longer cement products are wet, the stronger they become (FIG. 4-3).

4-3 Moisture barrier is applied to the rough top before installing the lath.

METAL LATH

Metal lath is sold in sheets measuring 26 × 8 feet. Chicken wire (poultry netting), which works just as well, can also be used. Whether you use lath or chicken wire, the reinforcing provides continuity, and mortar will not hold together without it. Lath can be nailed or stapled to the rough top through the moisture barrier. Fasteners should be 6 inches apart in both directions, and the pieces overlapped by at least 2 inches. I hold the lath back about ¼ inch from the edge of the counter so it won't get in the way of the trim pieces (FIG. 4-4).

4-4 Metal lath.

WOOD EDGE TREATMENT

As a design feature, finished wood boards are sometimes used for the counter edges instead of ceramic "shapes." This is where you woodworkers will shine. I've seen all types of hardwood and some softwoods used as decorative edge. The boards are applied to the edges of the tops and held to the proposed height of the finished tile. The tiles are then set snugly against the edge boards. Stained, varnished, or painted, wood lends an attractive contrast to tile. It also makes the work easier for the tile setter. If you plan on doing the edges in wood, do it before the tile process begins. The wood must be completely finished before tile work begins to seal out any water that might come in contact with it. Some woods, especially oak, turn black when they come in contact with water and cement. Installing wood edges is depicted in FIG. 4-5.

I've carried the wood treatment a step further in my home. The edges of our eating bar are done in white pine, which has been inlaid with long narrow strips of black ceramic tile. Let your imagination be your guide, but don't get carried away (FIG. 4-6).

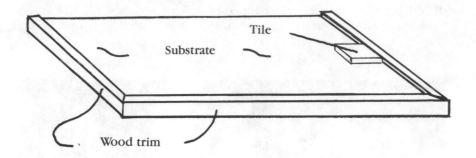

Tile

Substrate

Wood trim

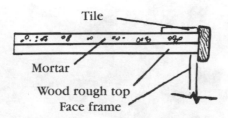

Tile

Mortar

Wood rough top

Face frame

4-5 Wood edge treatment.

4-6 Wood edge inlaid with tile.

GETTING STRAIGHT

Before mortar can be applied to countertops, there must be something to work to. The easiest thing to do is nail temporary "grounds" to the edges of the rough top, leveling them at the proposed height of the finished mortar. These can be pieces of wood boards ripped to about 2 inches in width, wood lattice, or just about anything that is not too wide and will provide a straight edge to work to. I've nailed my float strips to the edges of counters on more than one occasion. (See FIGS. 4-7 and 4-8.)

4-7 Level the grounds.

When nailing grounds on a countertop, determine the highest point on the counter and begin there, allowing about $3/4$ of an inch for mortar at that point. You can pre-start the nails into the strip, spacing them about 10 to 12 inches apart. Holding a 4-foot level on top of the strip, tack it to the edge of the rough top. Make sure there are no bends or bows in the strips. Whether the cabinets are in line or not, the counter edge must be straight. Remember that strips are not a permanent part of the installation, so don't drive nails in all the way.

The idea is to provide a straight, level surface that a straightedge can be held against while floating mortar on the top. You've noticed I haven't assumed that your cabinets are set level, and they probably aren't, but if by chance they are, you should allow for about $3/4$ of an inch of mud throughout the top.

4-8 Wood grounds completed.

FLOATING OUT OF LEVEL

As is sometimes the case with floors, drain boards can be so far out of level that it's not feasible to level them with mortar. This situation usually arises in very old homes which, through the years, have settled. I would say that if the counter is more than 1/2 inch out of level, it's best to "go with the flow." The "reveal," or distance between the bottom edge of the finished top and the tops of drawers and doors, has to be considered. If the counter is level and the face frames of the cabinets, along with the drawers and doors, are 1 inch out of level, the visual effect will not be acceptable. If everything else in the kitchen is out of whack, make the drain boards conform to the scheme. Just make sure you build the surfaces straight (on plane).

If you've opted for the wood edge method, obviously, the grounds aren't used. A screed can be formed at the front of the counter behind the wood trim to guide the straightedge. I'll discuss building screeds later in this section, but generally, screeds are built so that the surface of the tile is flush with the top edge of the wood trim.

MASKING

I usually mask off the fronts of cabinets with poly and masking tape. It is also a good idea to cover the floor. I'm probably one of the neatest tile setters and I still end up making a mess every time. While you're at it, cover the inside of the sink cabinet—you'll be dropping mortar through the hole where the sink goes.

Now might be a good time to stand around a while—the fun is about to begin. (See "Standing around," chapter 4.)

Chapter 15

Countertop layout

I know I've gone through layout in previous chapters, but proper layout is the most important element in the successful completion of any tile project. And in the case of a countertop, the project must be considered as a whole. There are no closets or cabinet toe spaces where unsightly cuts can be hidden. To the contrary, every little cut is not only visible, but intrinsic to the entire scheme. Balance is important in the sink area, especially if there is a window above the sink. Square tiles laid square to the wall must line up with the tiles on the back splash. At the same time, it's desirable to have the same size cuts on either side of the window opening, although this is not always feasible. What I'm driving at is that, unlike a floor where there might be several layout options, a countertop allows little or no leeway. There are definite starting points and very little room for improvisation.

STRAIGHT COUNTERS

In older kitchens, counters are sometimes straight, with no offsets or turns, and the sink is usually located someplace in the middle under the window. If you are tiling the counter only, no back splash, the logical thing to do is start at both ends with full tiles and work towards the sink. There are no full pieces of tile behind or in front of a sink anyway. Cuts behind the sink can be cut again when they reach the center of the opening, and the faucet will hide them. At the front, there are usually no tiles at all—only trim pieces.

If the back splash is also to be tiled, however, you're faced with a problem. The tiles on the splash must line up with the tiles on the counter and the cuts must run up the wall. This still might be the best way to go, but maybe not. It might be better to arrange the tiles on the splash so that they are centered on the window opening and the sink, and then make the counter line up with the splash. This would definitely be the thing to do if the counter abuts walls at both ends.

Another solution would be to turn the tiles on the counter diagonally so they won't have to line up with the splash. In many instances, this is what has been done through the years to solve the problem. With one exception, the first course of tiles at the front edge of the counter is always made up of full pieces. The cuts are made at the back against the splash. The exception is some eating bars that form a two-edged counter. In this case, the field might be shifted to provide for equal or more pleasing cuts at both edges.

L-SHAPED COUNTERS

Few modern kitchens contain straight counters. Most of them have offsets. Keeping in mind that the leading course of tile is always full, how are you going to accommodate the turn—the L? There is only one solution. Start in the corner—the L—and work in both directions from there.

What about the sink? It doesn't take a rocket scientist to figure out that you've lost control over the balancing of the cuts in that area. For the time being, let's hope the cuts at the sink area aren't skinny and that they'll still be pleasing to the eye.

U-SHAPED COUNTERS

Now you're getting into the big leagues. You now have two Ls to deal with, and because you are compelled to start both of them with a full piece of tile, there's a good possibility you are going to run into serious trouble at the sink area. Well, you're mud men (or women), remember? And if the project wasn't challenging, it wouldn't be any fun.

THE DUTCHMAN

There is no sense in getting too worried about what happens at the sink because there's very little tile there. The big concern is how to balance the back splash because its tiles must line up with those on the counter. So, you're coming along from both sides of the sink, and you get to the center behind the sink. One of two things is going to occur. You're either going to have a gap so narrow that a full tile won't fit into it or you'll have a wider gap that won't accommodate two pieces of tile. This is where the "dutchman" comes in.

Don't ask me where the term comes from, but a dutchman is a cut piece of tile used to fill in a gap when you've run tile from opposite directions and a full tile won't work in the remaining space. The dutchman is placed directly behind the sink opening. If the remaining space is wider than one full tile, a "double dutchman" is used . . . two pieces of tile cut to the same size. Another place this might be done is behind a built-in range top.

You always have the option of turning the tiles on the deck diagonally to the splash, but this constitutes a basic design change. In this case, the tiles at the front of the counter would be alternating full and half pieces.

In any case, the layout must be started from the L. There's no other way—unless there are to be cuts at the front edge of the counter—and with the one exception previously mentioned, this is not an acceptable design feature, nor is it technically correct.

Read along, and I'll discuss the solutions to these problems as they occur. There's always a way out.

Chapter 16

Floating counters

*F*loating a countertop, or drain board, is similar to floating a floor, only easier. The grounds are already in place so all that's left to do is get the mud in there and level it off—but not quite. Some type of level surface running down the length of the back splash to guide the other end of the straightedge is still needed. Yes, you're going to need a screed. If you haven't already read the section on mud work in chapter 4, please do so now. Pay particular attention to screed building and mixing mortar (deck mud).

Because countertops are horizontal surfaces, you'll be using deck mud to float them. Deck mud and floor mud are one and the same. Deck mud doesn't hold together well at the edges, however, so you're also going to use a little fat mud to go around the perimeter of the counter. *Fat mud* is another term for wall mud, the mortar mixed with lime.

Fat mud is mixed exactly like the mud used to float a tub splash in chapter 10 except not as much water is added. The mud must be very stiff—no slump. It can be mixed in a bucket but it's easier to use a wheelbarrow and a hoe. You didn't read about mixing mortar in chapter 10? Back you go again.

The amount of fat mud needed depends on the amount of counter to be floated, but usually, a bucket-full does it in the average kitchen. Place the mortar around the perimeter of the counter against the grounds and pack it in with a trowel. The mud border need only be a couple of inches wide. Allow it to remain slightly above the top edges of the grounds—you'll strike it off later, along with the deck mud. What you're doing is forming a firm border that won't slump or disintegrate when the wood grounds are removed (FIG. 4-9).

Of course, if your counter edges are trimmed with wood boards, you won't need fat mud at the edges. It is, however, required around the sink opening and the opening for the cook top, if any. It can also be used to float the windowsill.

4-9 Applying fat mud to the edges.

SINK OPENINGS

Grounds can be nailed to the inside of a sink opening and leveled with the grounds on the counter edges. The strips are cut to fit inside the opening, and then fat mud is packed against these grounds. I usually omit the grounds in this area and simply pack fat mud around the opening. The mud is then leveled with the ground on the front of the counter. Use your level as a straightedge and watch the bubble. Take pains to ensure that the opening in the mortar conforms to the sink opening in the rough top. Some sinks allow very little latitude. If you've installed a new plywood rough top, you can use the sink cutout as a template. This process is shown in FIGS. 4-10 and 4-11.

And now it's time to mix a little deck mud. You're not floating the kitchen floor, so don't get carried away. Ten shovels of sand in a wheelbarrow will get you started. Add two heaping shovels of portland cement and dry mix. Remember the sand castle consistency I talked about in chapter 4? This is what you're looking for, so easy on the water.

Why not simply float the entire countertop with fat mud? Well, for one thing, fat mud contains too much water, which will immediately float to the surface when the mud is worked with a trowel. Consequently, you end up floating water instead of mortar. Floating mortar is similar to finishing concrete. The water gets in the way, and when it has evaporated, the surface shrinks. Shrinkage might not be a consideration when finishing a concrete floor, but it certainly is when dealing with a countertop.

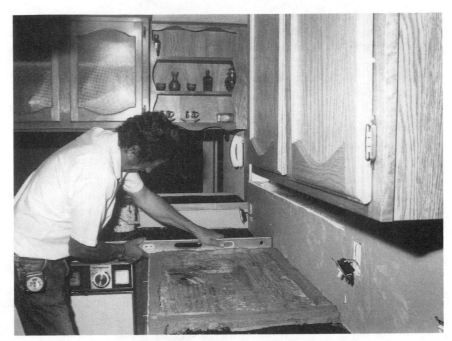

4-10 Roughing in the sink area.

4-11 Level the mud behind the sink opening.

Second, fat mud contains lime, which makes it sticky and hard to work to the smooth, consistent surface necessary when doing drain board work. The "cling factor" is only needed when floating walls because gravity is working against you. I've tried using fat mud on horizontal surfaces, and you can save yourself a lot of time and frustration by mixing the deck mud.

WINDOWSILLS

When a back splash is tiled, the windowsill over the sink is often also covered with tile. There are practical as well as aesthetic reasons for doing this. The sill can be more easily cleaned and condensation from the window pane will no longer pose a problem—it also looks good.

Tiling the sill is simple if your window is of the aluminum sash variety or if it's a steel casement window. The sill on this type of window is usually just nailed to the framing members and caulked against the sash. If this is the case, removing it poses no problem, although care should be taken not to damage the inside of the opening—the side jambs. Once the sill is removed, cover the sub-sill (2 × 4 framing) with a moisture barrier and lath, and float it with mortar when you float the counter. Because a sill is narrow, fat mud holds together better than deck mud. A straight-edge nailed across the opening at the appropriate height can help to keep the sill straight and level. Unlike a sill in a shower area, a kitchen windowsill is floated level (FIGS. 4-12 and 4-13).

4-12 Level the straightedge at the sill. Tack it in place with nails driven into the sheetrock (or cement board).

4-13 Floating the sill.

If your windows are made of wood and are of the vintage, double-hung sash variety, I would not recommend trying to tile the sill. Usually, the sill of a wood sash window forms an intrinsic part of the window frame and cannot be removed without removing the entire window from the opening. In this case, it's better to consider replacing the window with a new one than trying to remove only the sill. If a wood sill is to remain, however, you can remove the "apron" under it and tile right up to the bottom of the sill.

SCREEDS

Screeds are generally needed the entire length of the counter where it abuts the back splash. The exception would be an isolated section of cabinet, 2 to 3 feet wide, where grounds have been nailed to both ends. If a straightedge will reach from side to side, a screed isn't needed. Likewise, fat mud already applied behind the sink opening forms a screed, which should be leveled off at the same height as the ground at the front edge of the counter.

To begin building your screeds, dump a path of deck mud along the back of the counter against the back splash. The screed need be only 3 or 4 inches wide but high enough to level off with the ground at the front edge of the counter. Tamp the mortar down with a flat trowel until it is compacted. Using the level as a straightedge, wear the surface of the mud down to the exact level of the grounds. Check yourself by extending the level from the screed to the ground at the front edge of the counter. (See FIG. 4-14.)

4-14 Level the screeds at the splash.

Work your way along the entire length of the counter, keeping an eye on the bubble. The screed should be level, with no dips or humps, and at the same height as the grounds. Cut any excess mortar off with a flat trowel to form a clean line at the splash. Once the screeds are built, you're ready to fill the remainder of the surface with mud and level it off with a straightedge.

At this point, it doesn't matter where you start. You can begin at one end and work to the other or start at the sink area and work in either direction. Fill the area with deck mud, push it around, and tamp it down with the trowel. The filled area must be slightly higher than the grounds and the screed.

With a 2- or 3-foot straightedge held on the edge between the ground and the screed, begin scraping the mortar down. Don't try to scrape off too much mud at one time. Be very careful not to put a dip in the screed. As the mud builds up in front of the straightedge, remove it with a flat trowel (FIGS. 4-15 through 4-18).

When you have an area leveled, check for voids and fill them. You can check for humps by turning the straightedge parallel with the splash. A 4-foot level works best. When you're satisfied everything is in order, lightly smooth the entire surface with a flat trowel. Notice I said "lightly." Excessive pressure can cause a dip in the surface, causing the dreaded ski chute. When floating floors, small depressions are usually not a serious problem. Floor tiles are generally large enough to bridge small dips. Countertop tiles are usually much smaller, however, and humps and depressions are a far greater concern.

Continue floating the entire counter. Don't get in a hurry. This phase of the project is almost complete. Remember, you're a mud man (or woman) and it'll soon be time for another enjoyable period of "Standing around" or "Sitting around."

4-15 Using the straightedge. Keep an eye on the screed.

4-16 Pulling in the other direction.

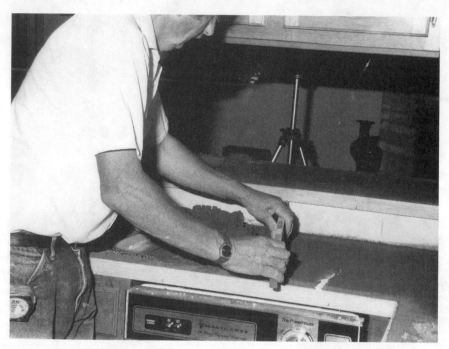

4-17 Don't put a dip in the screed—no "ski chutes."

4-18 Floating the eating bar.

When the entire project has been floated, go back once more and smooth the surface. A professional would probably begin setting the tile as soon as the counter is floated, but it doesn't have to be that way. You could allow the surface to set overnight and resume the following day. There's really no hurry, of course, you'll be without a kitchen sink and maybe a range, but one more day won't matter.

WOOD EDGE TRIM

Floating countertops is different when wood edges are used. In place of the ground, you'll need one of two things: a screed running along the front edge behind the wood trim board or a very ingenious homebuilt tool. You can go to the trouble of building the mud screed if you want to, but first let me tell you about the tool.

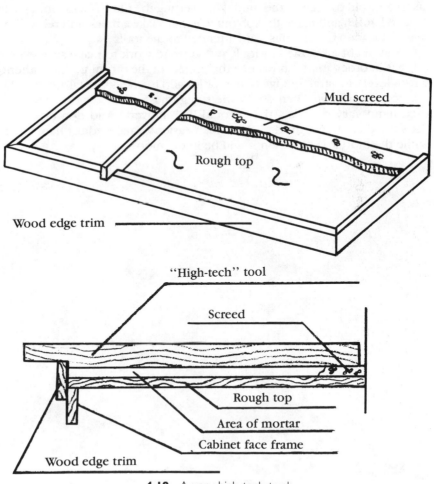

4-19 A very high-tech tool.

The wood trim has been installed straight and level, right? It could be used as a ground except it's too high; deck tiles must be set down flush with the trim. What you're going to need is a "trick stick." If you had a straightedge slightly longer than the depth of the counter when floating mud, and it had a notch in one end to ride on the trim board, you could drag the straightedge along, keeping an eye on the screed at the other end of it. And if the notch corresponds to the amount of mud you want to remove, it'll automatically keep the mud deck in exact conformity with the wood trim, which should be straight and level. Figure 4-19 shows you how to make this very "high-tech" tool. Before using it, it's advisable to run a strip of masking tape along the top of the trim board to prevent damaging your bright work.

Setting tile on drain boards is tedious but it's even more so when the mortar is fresh. The thin set must be mixed to the consistency of soup to avoid pulling mud from the deck when spreading it. Care must also be taken to avoid damaging the mud while setting the tile. So why not give it time to harden and make the job much easier? Take a break and relax after you've cleaned up the mess and attended to the tools.

You might take one last look at your mud work to make sure everything is in order and then resume the project in the morning. Use either a 4-foot level or a straightedge (4 feet or longer) to check the fairness of the horizontal surfaces. Then check the straightness of the edges. (If you've used temporary grounds, they should be removed.) And don't get the, "It's good enough attitude." It's much easier to make adjustments now while the mortar is wet then it will be in the morning.

Chapter **17**

Setting the tile

*T*he first pieces to be set are the trim pieces, or shapes at the front of the counter. If the trims are "sink rails," A-8262. With other types of trims, the field tiles might be set first. These pieces are 6 inches in length and generally don't line up with the field tile on the deck. Wall tiles measure $4^{1}/4$ inches square, and other tiles are not made to conform to the size of these trims, except for 6×6 standard wall tile. In the case of 6-inch wall tile with matching 6-inch trim, the field and trim are set more or less simultaneously. If you're using mosaics or other tiles with matching trim pieces, these must also be set simultaneously in order to keep the joints in line.

Which should be set first, the deck or the splash? Common sense would dictate tiling a splash before a deck. You wouldn't have to worry about making a mess on the deck while doing the wall. If the splash is not to line up with the deck, this is definitely the way to do it. If the splash and deck must align, however, the deck is usually done first. As I explained, layout options on a deck are severely limited—there are fixed starting points. Therefore, you should tile the counter first, establishing the lines that will dictate the final layout of the back splash.

INSTALLING SINK RAIL

A-8262 sink rail, also referred to as *V* cap, can be used as a trim for any type of countertop tile. Generally, the cap can be laid out along the length of each segment of the counter edge and shifted back and forth to determine the size of the cuts at the ends of the segments. The cuts aren't necessarily balanced from one end to the other; rather, the most eye-appealing arrangement is sought (FIG. 4-20).

Corner pieces, both inside and outside, are available for A-8262 and should be used. It's possible to miter the corner cuts on a tile saw, but the results are less pleasing. AN-8262 is the outside corner. The inside corner is AM-8262.

4-20 A cut at each corner.

Radii

Radius corners and curved edges should be avoided in ceramic tile. For one thing, edge trims are not available for curves unless they are custom made. Consequently, trim shapes must be mitered around the turn. They are cut into segments, the length of which depends on the radius of the turn. To me, the arrangement acquires a "butchered" look no matter how carefully the work is done.

The effect is not unpleasing, however, if mosaics are used, particularly 1 × 1s. Small pieces can be made to conform to a fairly tight radius without having to cut them.

So what it boils down to is: if mosaics are to be used, no problem, but if the pieces are going to be larger, do away with the radius. If possible, rebuild a portion of the counter and convert it into a square corner. The outside corner, AN-8262, is rounded and will take the sharpness out of the turn. Again, this is a design decision, and I'm not the designer.

U-shaped counters

By far the most difficult counter to lay out and tile is the U-shaped counter. If you can master this project, you'll be able to do just about any other counter.

Let's assume that there is an elevated eating bar at one side of the U and a raised counter at the other side above the range, which I'll deal with later. Also assume that standard 4¼ with corresponding A-4200 for the splash, sink rail (A-8262) for the deck trim, and 8 × 8 floor tiles laid diagonally for the decks will be used. The A-8262 will be installed starting at the outside corners and work will progress from there.

First, set the pieces "dry" to determine how the cuts are going to look. Set the outside corners, AN-8262, onto the counter. Be careful not to bump them off while you're working. Lay the caps along the edge of the counter, starting from the corners, working your way either to another outside corner or to the inside corners. Space them the width of the desired grout joints, usually about 1/16 inch.

Generally, the pieces abutting outside corners are not cut. Cuts are made at the inside corners unless it is determined that they would be too small—2 inches or less. If cuts would be too small, the piece next to the outside corner should be cut and the entire row shifted to allow for a larger cut at the L. The cut ends always go against the corner pieces and they are rubbed off with a rubbing stone to take the sharpness off the glaze. Be careful not to wear them down too much.

An exception to this rule occurs at the end of an eating bar where two outside corners are used. The cuts on this edge should be balanced and a cut placed adjacent to both outside corners (FIG 4-20). The same situation occurs at the bottom segment of the U where two inside corners form the limits. These pieces should also be balanced from one end of the segment to the other.

Remember, there are two ways of centering tiles or trim. A piece can be placed astride the centerline or you can have a grout line at the centerline with a piece of tile at either side. Do whatever allows the largest cuts. Don't end up with "skinnies."

Before you begin actually installing the pieces, remember it makes a difference what type of tile is going to be used on the deck. The thickness is a concern.

Matching wall tiles

If standard wall tiles are to be set square on the deck with their factory edges against the backs of the cap, no problem; you can set the trim, keeping it straight and level as you go. If the deck is to be set diagonally, however, there will be cut edges against the backs of the caps. These cut edges will protrude above the trim pieces because of the greater thickness of the wall tiles at their centers. It'll be necessary to "butter up" the trim pieces so they'll come up to the cut edges. Cut a piece of tile in half and use the cut edge as your guide. Slide the piece along the counter as you set the trim pieces. Allow an additional 1/16 inch in height for the thin set that will be under the deck tiles when they are set.

Mosaic tiles

Mosaics and other porcelain tiles will be thinner than the caps, and this poses no problem. Go ahead and set the trims, keeping them as low to the deck as possible. They still have to be set straight.

Floor tiles

Some floor tiles are much thicker than the trim pieces. The thin set used to set these trims must be mixed extremely thick—as thick as you can get it—thicker than peanut butter. Using a floor tile as your guide, set the trims. Remember, the tiles on the deck will be set in thin set and they'll be a little higher.

Setting A-8262, or any shaped trim, is not the easiest thing I've ever done. The vertical surfaces must be kept plumb, the pieces must be kept level and at the same time the trim must be set in a straight line. But can you handle it? You bet, you're mud men!

A 4-foot level (or a straightedge) is a definite necessity. The trims are buttered with a buttering trowel or a margin trowel. Butter both surfaces, vertical and horizontal, and set a row 3 or 4 feet long beginning with a corner piece and the cut adjacent to it. Now, use the straightedge to go back and see what you've done. Use the straightedge to check the horizontal and vertical surfaces for alignment. Individual pieces will have to be reset.

The next step is to set a row on the other side of the same corner. This will ensure that the corner piece has been set squarely in both directions. Pieces can be moved back and forth slightly until they are properly aligned. The cuts can then be made at the ends of each segment. Remem-

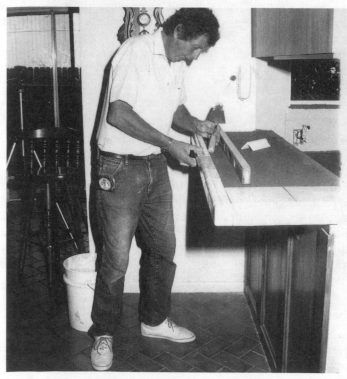

4-21   Installing V cap (sink rail).

ber, the fronts must be straight and vertical, or plumb. Don't get in a hurry. When the trims are set, the rest of the work is easier (FIGS. 4-21 through 4-26).

If other trim pieces are to be used, they are set at the same time as the deck tiles because alignment of the grout joints is essential each step of the way.

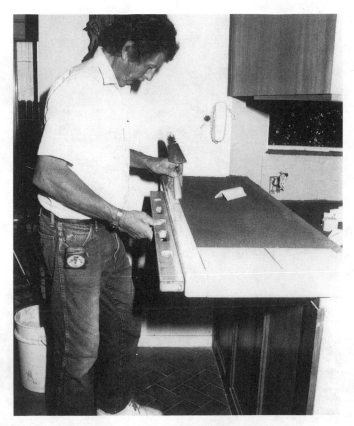

4-22 Using the level as a straightedge.

SETTING THE DECK TILES

By now, the resident chef wants the kitchen sink installed and things are heating up around the work site. Again, my only advice is: keep your composure and encourage the chef to do the same. A gourmet dinner at a nice restaurant might be an acceptable consolation.

The size of the notched trowel is determined by the backs of the tiles to be set. If they're relatively smooth (wall tiles, mosaics, and porcelains), a 1/8- or 3/16-inch notched trowel should be used. Floor tiles usually have some sort of grid pattern on their back sides and a trowel with larger notches will be needed. While we want the tiles to be well bonded, we don't want thin set squeezing up through the grout joints.

4-23 Backing up the level with the "old eyeball."

4-24 Start at the outside corner and work toward the U.

4-25 We are mitering the inside corners because the corner pieces were not available when the tile was purchased.

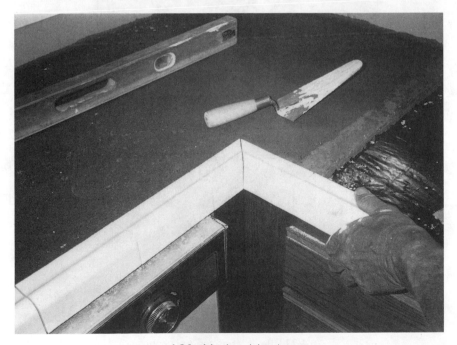

4-26 Moving right along.

The thin set must be creamy, not stiff or runny. We'll want the ridges formed by the trowel to reach up and grip the bottoms of the tiles but the thin set must still be workable. Don't mix a large batch. It doesn't take a lot to do the job, and the work doesn't go that fast. A third of a bucket will do.

If you're using mosaics, or other tiles that are thinner than the trim pieces, you'll need to use a slightly larger notched trowel and fairly stiff thin set. This allows you to raise the field tiles closer to the level of the trims. It doesn't hurt to leave the tiles a little lower than the trims, however, as long as the effect is continuous throughout the installation.

Smear an area in one of the Ls, from the corner to the back splash. An area of about 4 to 6 square feet can be covered. Watch for overglazing. As you'll recall, overglazing occurs when the thin set begins to dry on its surface after being spread and tiles will not bond to it properly. Therefore, don't spread an area larger than you can cover with tile in about five minutes (FIG. 4-27).

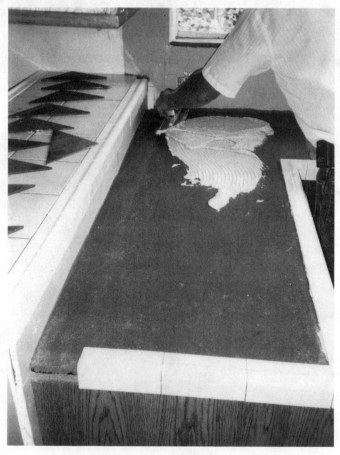

4-27 Begin at an inside corner.

Whether your tiles are individual pieces or mounted on sheets makes no difference. The starting point remains the same. A piece of tile must be located in the L so that a full row of tiles will go down the two legs of the counter at its front edge (FIG. 4-28). The exception for the eating bar still applies.

4-28 This is the starting point.

SETTING TRIM PIECES

When trims correspond in size to deck tiles, they are set at the same time. Mosaic trims are usually attached to each other in strips of several tiles—"stretchers." Stretchers are laid along the edge of the counter and aligned with the deck tiles. The trims must overhang the edge so that the vertical pieces to be attached later will be flush with them. The same holds true for individual pieces of trim. Align them with the field tiles and allow them to overhang the edge. Use a piece of tile held against the vertical edge as a gauge. It's a little tricky getting started but it goes fairly smoothly after that.

When all the full tiles have been set, it's time to put in the cuts at the splash. Make sure your thin set has not overglazed. If it has, butter a skim coat of thin set on the back of each cut. Don't build the cuts up to a higher level than the full pieces adjacent to them (FIG. 4-29). When the first area is complete, tap the tiles in with the beater block and a trowel handle. Don't use a hammer, you're just making sure the tiles are level with each other. And if you've used a larger notched trowel to raise the tiles, tap very gently. Don't push them down into the thin set, just get them level with each other. If you've moved them, you can push against their edges with a trowel to get them back in place (FIG. 4-30).

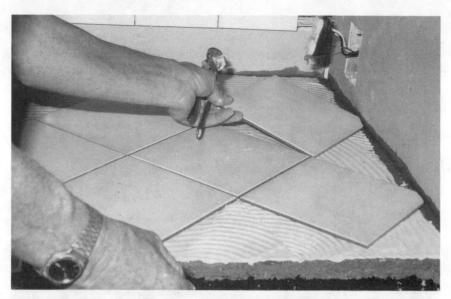

4-29 Install the cuts last.

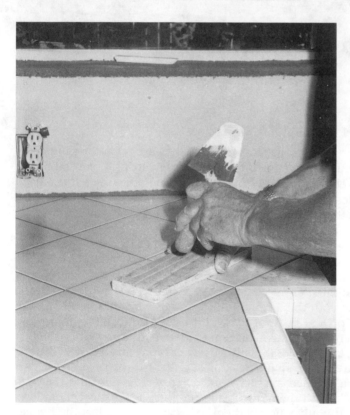

4-30 Tap gently.

The field is now worked in either direction and all cuts are made and installed. Work small areas at a time and tap the tiles in as you go. If your tiles don't have spacer lugs on their edges, a carpenter's square can be laid on the deck to help keep them aligned and square. Line up one leg of the square with the counter edge and the other with a grout line in the field.

When the sink area is reached, make the cuts that go along the end of the opening and then the rounded L cuts in the corners of the sink. These cuts can be made with biters. Be sure that the cut edges are directly above, and in line with, the opening. Some sinks, stainless steel ones in particular, allow very little variance (FIG. 4-31). Don't worry about the small cuts along the front and back sides of the opening at this time. These cuts will be installed after the counters at both ends of the opening have been tiled.

4-31 The cuts at the end of the sink opening.

Repeat the process in the other corner of the U, and work in either direction (FIG. 4-32). The thing to remember is that a full piece of tile goes in the corner and the leading rows of tile along the front edges of the counter must be full tiles—no cuts. Please forgive me for repeating myself; it's important.

4-32 Work in either direction from the U.

RANGES

Openings for built-in ranges can be treated like sink openings. The difference is the wall at the splash is higher and a dutchman will be more noticeable in this area. If the splash is to be lined up with the deck, it's best to maintain the layout on the deck. In other words, you must work across the opening and keep the proper spacing. This can be done by measuring across the opening. Measure a row of tiles set elsewhere on the deck and transfer the measurement to the front edge of the counter at the range opening.

The same situation occurs with a full-size range. The counters are separated but the splash is not. You must measure across the opening to determine where the tile is to be placed on the counter farthest from the L. Another method is to delay tiling the far counter until the back splash is tiled. As you're tiling behind the range, the placement of the tiles on the unfinished deck will be apparent.

But back to the sink opening. The cuts at the front (if any) and the back of the opening can now be set. Start from both sides with full-length pieces and work to the center. The remaining gap at the center will be filled with either a dutchman or a double dutchman. If the gap is slightly narrower than a full tile, a dutchman is used. If it is wider than a full tile, a double dutchman is used. Unless you are very lucky, the cut or cuts will be slightly off center, but this won't be noticeable. The remaining deck areas are then tiled and cuts are made at the ends (FIGS. 4-33 and 4-34).

4-33 Tiling the bar.

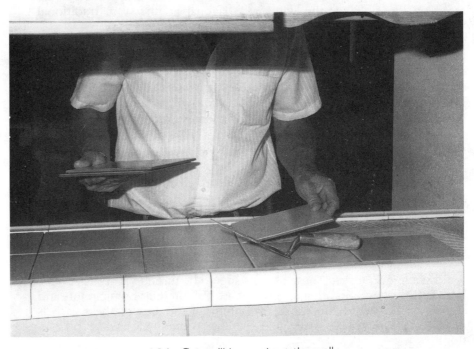

4-34 Cuts will be made at the wall.

Are we finished with the deck? Almost. Let's go back and make a final check before we get on with the splash. It's much easier now than when the thin set has dried and hardened.

1. The field tiles are set level (no "hangers").
2. Visible cuts are pleasing.
3. Layout begins at the inside corners of the counter.
4. Edge trim is level and straight.

If you haven't used A-8262 or wood trim, the vertical pieces at the counter edge should be placed at this time. The pieces can be held up to the surface trim with bits of masking tape to keep them from sagging. If they are attached to sheets, stretchers can be cut to match the surface trim. Remember to allow a grout joint between these pieces and the surface cap and align the vertical joints with those on the surface. Because these edge pieces will be attached to wood as well as mortar, multipurpose thin set should be used. An alternative would be to make a small batch of thin set using latex instead of water. Nothing to it.

DIAGONALS

As I've mentioned, the problems of aligning the deck with the splash can be eliminated by turning the tiles on the deck diagonally to the splash (as we've done). The splash can then be treated as a separate project, and it can be done before or after the deck. The field in the sink area can be centered on the sink—or the window. Diagonal counters are traditional when a more informal look is desired.

It is still essential to start the layout in the bends of the counter—the Ls. The course adjacent to the edge trim will be made up of alternating full tiles and halves cut diagonally. The skinny cuts behind the sink can be square cuts. These cuts are hardly noticeable in any case. And if it is determined that the cuts on either side of the sink will be unsightly, a square border can be set. The diagonal halves at the front of the counter must be cut precisely. A tile saw helps, but if you don't have one, the cuts can be made on a tile cutter. The cut edges are then rubbed with a stone (FIG. 4-35).

SETTING THE SPLASH

Before any work is done on the splash, precautions must be taken to avoid electrical shock. The switches and receptacles must be pulled from the junction boxes and taped with electrical tape.

In addition, most local building codes provide for separate circuits for kitchen receptacles. These circuits should be turned off at the service box. Dishwashers and other appliances are also on their own circuits and should be turned off. In short, everything in the area of the splash is turned off. Taping receptacles and switches is merely a backup precaution.

4-35 Sawing diagonals.

Setting the splash is much less tedious than setting the deck, provided no serious mistakes were made while tiling the counter. The vertical joints on the splash are aligned with the corresponding joints on the counter if the deck tiles are set square to the splash. In most cases, the bottom course of tile is left full, and the cuts are placed at the top, up under the cabinets where they won't be noticed. Because the layout is predetermined, it doesn't matter where you start. I usually start at either end and work to the sink area.

Layout options for the splash in the sink area are discussed further later in the chapter. In the meantime, don't smear this area with thin set until you've decided on your plan of attack. In our project, we'll center the splash at the window because the sink is not centered.

SETTING TILES ON SHEETS

Smear a small section, 2 or 3 feet long, with thin set. Don't forget about overglazing. If there are no electrical outlets in the way, place a sheet of tile at the end of the splash and align the joints with the counter. I use small nails driven through the joints into the wall to hold the sheets in place. A grout joint should be provided at the splash-deck juncture. Space must be left for the trim pieces that will finish off the end, and you might have a vertical row of cuts next to them. Set the first sheet accordingly.

Cutting around electrical outlets entails removing enough tiles from the sheet to accommodate the opening and then making the cuts and installing the pieces individually. To remove pieces from a sheet, turn the sheet over and cut the backing with a utility knife or a razor blade. The cuts can be held in place with masking tape. L cuts and other necessary cuts are discussed in Part 3.

SETTING STANDARD WALL TILE

These are the easiest tiles to install because they have spacer lugs built into their edges. The first, or bottom, course is set and the remaining courses are lined up above it. The cuts are made at the top under the upper cabinets. On our project, about 1 inch is cut off the bottom course to allow for more pleasing cuts near the eating bar. L cuts are required at electrical outlets and probably, at the window opening. Occasionally, U cuts are needed. Split cuts might be made, but this is usually not done on the kitchen splash. If you don't have a tile saw, and you're not able to make the cuts with biters, mark them and take them to your tile supply for cutting.

The trims used for wall tile are usually S-4269 (surface caps), along with their corners, SN-4269 (outside) and SM-4269 (inside). If cement backer board was used on the splash (or an additional layer of sheetrock), the trims will be A-4200. The corners are AN-4200 (outside) and AM-4200 (inside). Caps will be needed at the ends of the splash and at the window area.

4-36 The gourmet dinner.

SETTING OTHER TILES

Plastic spacers are available at tile supplies to facilitate setting tiles that do not have spacer lugs. The plastic spacers are a definite plus. They are inserted after each course, and the subsequent course is then set. The spacers should be removed prior to grouting the installation. Bits of cardboard, toothpicks, and plastic wedges can also be used.

NOTE: Handmade tiles or tiles of irregular shape cannot be set with spacers. Some other method must be devised, i.e., shims, wedges, etc.

The use of floor tiles on the splash is becoming common. It must be noted, however, that electrical outlets might fall in the center of larger pieces. In this case, a closed cut (a hole) must be made, which can get a little tricky. I would suggest you mark these cuts and take them to your tile supplier to be cut. You needn't interupt your work—they can be installed later.

SETTING SPLASH ENDS

If the splash must line up with the deck, you have no control over the joint layout of the splash but you do have a couple of options of where it ends. In the case of eating bars, the upper cabinets don't generally line up with the edge of the counter. In this case, a "return" is possible (FIG. 4-37).

4-37 One end of the splash.

Or, you might elect to end the splash even with the upper cabinet. Where an upper cabinet is in line with its corresponding base cabinet, however, there really are no options. The splash is stopped even with the cabinets. By now I'm sure you can appreciate the advantages of running the deck diagonally and not having to align the splash with it.

Let's assume we're going to have some cuts at the end of the splash—there's no way around it. We'll start at one end and hope for the best. The field tiles are set first, the cuts are made and installed, and the end trims are set. As you're working along, take care to keep the courses straight and level. If you smear small areas at a time, there'll be no hurry. The work will not go fast because of the obstructions to be cut around. Take your time. Another gourmet dinner perhaps?

SINK AREA

If your splash must line up with the counter, you've got to figure out what to do behind the sink. Whatever you end up with, it should be centered—either on the sink opening or on the window opening (sometimes the two aren't in line) (FIG. 4-38).

4-38 We've centered the field on the window opening.

DESIGN FEATURES

If the dutchman mentioned earlier doesn't appeal to you, you might try getting really tricky and incorporate a design into the wall behind the sink. You might stop at both sides and turn the field in the remaining space on the diagonal, for example. Or, you might find some decorative tiles of a different size, and center them behind the sink. The design might be carried to other areas of the splash. This is where true creativity comes into play.

The design feature doesn't necessarily have to continue onto the window sill, and the trim pieces at the sill can be centered in the opening. There are a number of possibilities, and new ones are created every day. You are the designer, and you're certainly not in a great hurry. You can experiment—but can you really afford another gourmet dinner?

WINDOW OPENING

Trim pieces at the opening are usually placed on the wall side, i.e., the surface facing you and not on the inside of the opening. Outside corners are used at the top of the splash and inside corner pieces at the ends of the sill. (See FIG. 4-38.)

Whether you tile the side jambs of the opening is a matter of choice. In any case, the trims are set and adjusted first. The cuts are then made against them (FIG. 4-39). The last thing to be tiled is the horizontal surface of the sill itself.

You won't need my help in tiling the remaining walls. If the deck tiles are set diagonally or are of a different size than the tiles on the splash, you can start at the ends of the walls and work to the inside corners making your end cuts there. If, however, the tiles must be aligned with the deck, you can start and finish anywhere you like.

4-39 Tiling the sill.

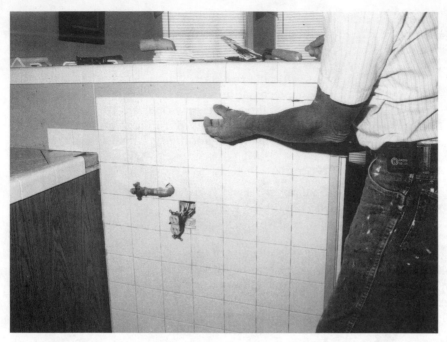

4-40 Behind the range (optional).

4-41 Tiling an end wall.

4-42 Another gourmet meal, anyone?

CLEANING UP

Before shims, masking tape, and spacers can be removed, the tile will have to set, usually for an hour or two. As soon as the tiles are firmly set, go back over the installation, remove the spacers, and wash the entire splash. If thin set is protruding through joints, it can be scratched out with the point of a nail. A margin trowel sometimes loosens the tiles. While you're at it, it won't hurt to give the deck one final check.

After you've cleaned your tools and buckets, take a break. The tile should not be grouted until the following day. As you'll recall, excess moisture in and around the tiles will have an adverse effect on the final shade of the grout. Waiting overnight ensures that moisture from the thin set has evaporated.

Chapter **18**

Grouting and sealing

Grouting counters and splashes is no different than grouting floors and walls. The same principles apply. If the grout joints are 1/8 of an inch wide or less, unsanded grout is used. If they are wider, sanded grout must be used. Porcelain mosaics, however, are usually grouted with sanded grout—it sets better in the joints. Because our installation contains both floor and wall tiles, both sanded and unsanded grout will be used.

Whether to use latex grout is another question. In my opinion, all counters and splashes should be sealed with penetrating masonry sealer. In this light, latex grout should not be used. Latex is, in itself, a semi-sealer and will inhibit the penetration of other sealers.

Why must the tile and grout be sealed? Several factors must be considered. The countertop is one of the most-used surfaces in the home and will be subjected to a variety of spills and stains. It is also subjected to closer scrutiny than a floor, for example. Life in many American homes evolves around the kitchen and the counter area is much closer to eye-level than other tiled surfaces, i.e., floors.

It's true, that many of the tiles commonly used on counters will not accept sealers—they're too dense—but the grout joints certainly will. The entire installation can be gone over with sealer and the sealer removed from tile surfaces with dry rags or paper towels.

EPOXY GROUT

I don't recommend using epoxy grout in the home for two reasons. First, I consider its use overkill—portland cement grout, properly sealed, will do the job nicely and it's much less expensive. Second, epoxy grout is much less forgiving than portland cement grout and its use requires a higher degree of expertise. There are new epoxys available that can be cleaned up with water—and that's a plus. Earlier epoxy grouts, which are

213

still used on commercial jobs, must be cleaned with special solvents. Grouting, in general, is a tedious process, and I see no reason to compound the issue.

In addition, there have been some problems reported concerning the newer epoxy grouts that are washed with water. Manufacturers claim that the problems are due to faulty application, but experienced installers are having difficulties with some of the products. There is at least a possibility that the products have not been fully developed. So for the time being, I'd stick with time-proven materials.

GROUTING A SPLASH

The splash is grouted before the deck for obvious reasons. Once the splash area is cleaned up, the counters are grouted, and the job is complete. Care must be taken at the wall-deck juncture. The grout is scraped flat. It is not left rounded. Use a flat screwdriver or a margin trowel to achieve a straight, consistent joint in this area. Wall junctures are treated the same way.

It is important to keep the grout joints as full as possible, so don't wash them down too much. Full, level joints not only present the optimum visual effect, they also facilitate cleaning. Food particles and other substances are less likely to become lodged in the joints. You might even consider re-grouting the deck after the first grout has set. In this case, you would re-grout as soon as the original grout becomes firm to the touch—two to four hours. If you wait too long, the additional grout will not form a proper bond.

You've spent a great deal of time preparing the surface and installing the tile, and grouting requires a relatively short period of time, but it absolutely makes or breaks the entire project. My "helper" demonstrates the technique in FIGS. 4-43 and 4-44.

SEALING

You must wait at least five days before sealing a ceramic installation. By that time, any moisture in the cement products will have, for the most part, evaporated. During the drying time, the surfaces must be protected from stains when used. At the same time, you won't want to cover the surface with anything that will inhibit the escape of the moisture. You can lay pieces of plastic sheeting on the counters when they are used—just be sure to remove it later so that the entire surface can dry (cure) at the same rate. I know, by now, you've re-installed the sink and the range. It's back to pot roast and meat loaf.

I like the old-fashioned penetrating sealers. It just seems to me that something that is not water-soluble will do a better job of repelling water than something that is water-soluble. Manufacturers and distributors will not agree, but I've never had much luck using latex-based sealers. In fact, the only advantage of using latex sealers is that they don't permeate the air with the strong paint smell associated with mineral-based products. I can put up with the smell for a day or so. I just do the job and leave.

4-43 Grout the splash first.

4-44 Don't wash it down too much.

Silicone sealer is the one to use. It's sold at home centers, paint stores, masonry supplies, and some tile supplies. Make sure you get the penetrating type and buy only a quart—it doesn't take much to do the job.

Because the area to be sealed is relatively small, the entire job can be done with a paint brush, a sponge, or both. Care must be taken around the edges of the splash, otherwise it just gets on the surface. Allow it to stand three or four minutes and then wipe off the excess. Completely dry the surfaces of the tiles. Continue along until the job is completed. Allow the surface to dry overnight and then repeat the process.

When using this type of sealer, plenty of ventilation must be provided, and when you're finished, get out for several hours. Read and adhere to the manufacturer's instructions on the container.

If you discover you've somehow left excess sealer on the tiles, you can remove it with a cloth dampened with paint thinner. Don't flood the area with thinner. Use as little as possible.

BATHROOM COUNTERS

Anyone who can tile a kitchen counter will have no problem in the bathroom, and there's not much more I can add. However, vanity tops seldom contain Ls, and centering the layout is usually not a problem. The front course of tile is set full and the cuts are made at the back.

Corner cabinets

If the cabinet has one open end, the tiles should be full at that end as well as at the front, if possible. An exception can be made if the cuts at the opposite wall will be too "skinny." In this case, the tiles at the open end should be cut off enough to allow more pleasing cuts at the wall.

Freestanding cabinets

If the cabinet stands in the middle of a wall and has two open ends, the field should be centered. Remember, there are two ways of centering: a full tile at the center or a grout joint on the centerline. Whichever arrangement allows for the largest cuts at the ends is the correct one. You could also start at both ends with full pieces, and work towards the sink—if it's centered. A dutchman can be used at the narrow areas in front of, and behind, the sink.

Enclosed cabinets

Counters that abut vertical surfaces on both ends are usually centered. However, the field might be centered on the sink instead, provided the sink is more or less centered in the top. Cuts at vertical surfaces (the ends of the counter) are less noticed than those at an open edge.

The splash

In most cases, bathroom splashes are very low and of little consequence but occasionally, the splash forms a continuation of a wainscot at an adjacent wall. In this case, the layout of the counter might be governed by the wainscot, but keep in mind the other options, i.e., a dutchman, design features, etc.

And now, my friends, we must part. I sincerely hope I've been able to help you with your endeavors. I've tried to answer all the questions, but I know that that would not be possible. There are always new questions. I suggest you become acquainted with the people at your tile supply, maybe even hang around awhile (not in the showroom, but in the back of the warehouse or in the yard). There is usually a coffee pot going most of the day, and tile setters and contractors come and go at steady intervals. I'll let you in on a little secret: most tile setters love to talk (I'm not the only one), and the talk is always about tile.

If only to demonstrate his superior knowledge, the setter is usually happy to answer the questions of a novice. And if you act really impressed, he'll tell you everything he knows.

When contemplating tile projects, impose no deadlines on yourself. Having fun is a big part of doing the work yourself. Plan your work schedule in segments and allow plenty of time for each segment. Remember, the work you are doing is permanent and the materials are expensive.

And yes, you're going to make mistakes, but don't let it slow you down. The measure of a good craftsman is not in the number of mistakes he might make—we all make them; rather, it is in how he corrects those errors and makes the job look right.

Happy tile setting!

Appendix

Repairing tile surfaces

*T*here are only two possible repairs that ceramic tile might require: replacing existing tiles or replacing existing grout.

REPLACING EXISTING TILES

Tiles can be removed from a field by first removing the grout that surrounds them. The grout must be removed so that the lateral pressure of removing the piece does not damage adjacent tiles. Grout saws, or scratchers, are sold at tile supplies, home hardware centers, and building supplies. A grout saw is a hand tool consisting of a handle to which a small blade is attached. The cutting edge of the blade is encrusted with carbide particles that wear away the grout. You can also break a hacksaw blade into segments and use them as grout saws for unsanded grout.

Wall tiles

Standard wall tiles are the hardest tiles to replace. The spacing lugs are wedged tightly together in the field. Though grout can be removed, the lugs still exert pressure on adjacent tiles. You must remove a wall tile in very small fragments. In fact, it's necessary to completely pulverize the piece. Start in the center of the piece and work toward adjacent tiles, removing small fragments as you go. When you get close to an adjacent tile, try to knock the fragments away from it. Do not drive a chisel toward the adjacent tiles. A very small masonry chisel (available at tile supplies) and a hammer will do the work.

Floor tiles

Floor tiles are much easier to replace because the grout joints are wider. You simply saw the grout down to the thin set, break the piece with a hammer, and remove the piece. Other tiles with wide joints fall into the same category.

Once the tile has been removed, clean the old grout from the edges of the adjacent tiles and remove the old thin set from the opening. The replacement piece can then be installed and grouted.

REPLACING EXISTING GROUT

Although tile might still be in good shape, it is not uncommon for the grout to be discolored. Shower areas are the most frequent victims and drain boards are another. Before you begin to remove the grout, the surface must be thoroughly cleaned. Soap scum and other grime must be completely removed from the surface.

The old grout does not have to be completely removed from the joints. It is sawn close to the spacer lugs of the wall tile to provide enough tooth for the new grout. Some wall tiles are set quite closely together, and a grout saw might mar the tiles themselves. This is when a hacksaw blade can come in handy. It's harder to use than a grout saw, but it is narrower. Once the floor tile joints are sawn down to about half their depth, use a vacuum cleaner to get all the dust out of the joints. The joints should then be dampened with water—not wet, just moist.

When tile is installed over nothing but sheetrock, hairline cracks sometimes form at the junctures of walls and decks. A classic example would be at the splash-deck juncture of our kitchen counter project. In this case, it's best to scratch out the grout and replace it with latex caulking. Buy the best caulking available. Caulking is available in various colors. The same is true of the juncture between a tub splash and the tub itself. Remove the grout and caulk it.

If the grout around a piece of tile begins to loosen and crack, it means the piece is loose. It won't do any good to replace the grout only. The piece must be removed and reset or replaced.

If a series of tiles form hairline cracks, it probably means there's a crack in the substrate. This happens most often on concrete floors. If the cracks aren't too unsightly, leave them alone. There's nothing that can be done about the underlying cause, and replacement tiles will probably crack also. It is possible, however, to replace the tiles using floor mastic instead of thin set. This will allow the replacement tiles to more or less "float" over the crack. You might still experience cracks along the grout lines, but they will be less unsightly than cracks in the tiles themselves. If the crack becomes serious, it could mean the floor is settling and foundation repairs might be in order.

On outdoor projects, if enough expansion joints have not been provided, it's possible for areas of the tile work to delaminate from the substrate—sections of tile that rise up from the concrete. This is caused by the different rates of expansion and contraction between various materials. New expansion joints can be sawn into the surface. To make repairs without providing new joints is folly. Call a concrete cutting contractor. You'll find them in the yellow pages. If you're not sure where the new joints should be cut, a concrete specialist will. When replacing outdoor tiles, use multipurpose thin set or mix regular gray thin set with latex instead of water.

In short, when tiles break or grout cracks for no apparent reason, determine the reason. You must cure the cause as well as the effect.

Grout stain

Some manufacturers of grout products make stains that match their grout colors. The word *stain* is a misnomer because the products are topical—they don't penetrate. In this light, the results are temporary, because the "stain" will eventually wear off the surface of the grout. I've never used these products, but if I did, I would use them to cover over small areas of discolored grout. I wouldn't consider going over an entire kitchen floor, for example.

Index